Chloe Sims

The Only Way Is Up

My Story

Chloe Sims

The Only Way Is Up
My Story

JOHN BLAKE

www.johnblakepublishing.co.uk

www.facebook.com/Johnblakepub facebook
twitter.com/johnblakepub twitter

First published in hardback in 2012

ISBN: 978 1 78219 042 4

British Library Cataloguing-in-Publication Data:

A catalogue record for this book is available from the British Library.

Design by www.envydesign.co.uk

Printed and bound in Great Britain by CPI Group (UK) Ltd

1 3 5 7 9 10 8 6 4 2

Papers used by John Blake Publishing are natural, recyclable products made from wood grown in sustainable forests. The manufacturing processes conform to the environmental regulations of the country of origin.

Every attempt has been made to contact the relevant copyright-holders, but some were unobtainable. We would be grateful if the appropriate people could contact us.

I'd like to dedicate this book to three of
the most important people in my life: my dad,
my daughter Madison and my Starship.

Contents

CHAPTER ONE

My Crazy Life

Being famous was never something I'd thought about – it certainly wasn't an ambition, like it is for some people.

The truth is, I wanted to be a model; I had never even thought for a minute about being on TV, but I needed cash and fame brings you money. It's as simple as that. I'd tried everything else, but I hadn't tried fame. Being on TV would give my daughter and me a better life.

I am a firm believer that, if you want something enough, then somehow you will get it. Many times over the years I have said to myself, 'This is not my real life' – as if I was not living the life I was meant to.

Finally, I feel as though I am.

For as long as I can remember, I've wanted a white Mercedes. I never thought in a million years I would get one, but now I have. I'm proud of it but also surprised that I have managed to bag my dream car. That's not just it, me and my seven-year-old daughter Madison, or Mady for short, moved into a new house at the beginning of this year, and we are really happy and settled. Before that, we lived in a flat on a main road, Queens Road, in Buckhurst Hill, and it was a nightmare.

We lived opposite a social club and it was really noisy – there would be people leaving late at night and it used to keep Mady awake. They would get deliveries at all hours and the sound of them rolling the barrels right past our front door used to make the whole place shake. Then there was Costa Coffee, which was next door – they would get deliveries at 4am every single day.

It's funny because it never really felt like home, even though we lived there for two-and-a-half years. I didn't even bother to finish decorating it because it always felt temporary.

Now we live on the edge of farmland, with a huge garden and stunning views across the countryside. Mady can go out and see the cows and sheep in the fields and there's no banging around at all hours – finally, we feel happy and safe.

I first heard about *The Only Way Is Essex* a couple of years ago when a gang of friends told me about this show that they were involved in. It was being made in Essex by a TV company called Lime Pictures.

They were wanting to film glamorous, larger-than-life characters that were well known on the party circuit for what sounded like an exciting new type of TV series – all glossy like a soap, but with real people. It was going to cover everything from bikini waxes to cheating and rows over men!

I hated my job and wasn't earning a lot of money at the time; I thought it could be a lifesaver for me, and it sounded like a laugh, too! They were holding auditions at Faces nightclub in Gants Hill and I knew the owner, Tony Bee, so I asked him for the producer's phone number. I thought about it for a while and then decided I had nothing to lose, so I eventually rang the number.

The producer was a woman called Sarah Dillistone, and we arranged to meet up in the King William pub in Chigwell. Over a drink, I told her about my crazy life and we chatted for hours. I told her about being single and the dating disasters I'd had, and she told me to email her over a short blog every week about what I'd been up to and any dates I'd been on.

After a couple of months of my sending over the weekly emails, Sarah rang me and asked if I was still interested but by then I'd just landed a new job that paid pretty well and things were starting to look up.

They wanted to come round to my house and film me, so I agreed to that. Afterwards, they still seemed keen and Sarah asked if I would do the show. It was only £50 a day to cover expenses, and I would have to do my own hair, make-up and styling, but I would be on the telly! She explained that, like with all successful shows, it could open up the doors to make personal appearances and interviews. She told me they thought it would be a real success, and I remember her saying, 'This could be really good for you,' and telling me it could well be my big break – but I started having second thoughts.

I had landed a job as a Playboy bunny and I felt I couldn't give that up. I was also told that filming would be continuous, so I wouldn't be able to be out of the country. At the time, I was working in France, so I felt I just couldn't do it.

I had no idea whether the show would be a success and I just felt it was too big a risk to take. I honestly didn't think it would be any good! Plus, I was worried that being on TV would mean my whole life would be scrutinised and picked apart. I was scared about what people would think of me – what if they all hated me and it ruined mine and Mady's lives?

I had a nice set-up with work, so I turned it down.

The show began in October 2010. I then realised what a massive mistake I had made. Every weekend, I was travelling backwards and forwards to France, and all the travelling was beginning to get right on my nerves.

On Fridays, I would drop Mady at school and drive to Stansted as quickly as I could to make the flight to wherever I was going that weekend. It was relentless – I was a single mum all week looking after Mady on my own and then I was working really long hours at weekends.

Sometimes our group of Playboy girls would land at the airport and then drive ten hours to a small French village and I was sick of it. I remember one morning when I was waiting for my flight to be called and I was looking in a newsagent's at all the gossip magazines. Every single one of them had the *TOWIE* girls on the front and it just hit me: I had made the biggest mistake of my life.

All I could think was: 'That could have been me' and I was devastated. That was it – I had missed my chance. I tried to put it out of mind because there was no point in dwelling on it: I had made my choice, and that was that.

Then, in early 2011, I had a call from my friend Layla Manoochehri, whose boyfriend was Simon Webbe from the boy band Blue. She had also been in talks to appear on the show, and she told me the *TOWIE* producers were trying to get in touch with me. I couldn't believe it – I'd tried to forget all about it and put all thoughts of *TOWIE* behind me, and I didn't dare think what this could mean.

I phoned them and spoke to the new producer, Katie Fox, who asked me in for a chat. She told me they were seeing if people they had spoken to before Series One were still interested in joining the show – they wanted to bring in some new faces for the second series. I told her I'd love to. She explained they would send a cameraman to my house and film me, and then they had to send the footage to ITV to see if I was suitable, and it turned out I was! The next step was a meeting with some bigwigs from ITV and the production company, Lime Pictures.

By this point, I was determined that I was going to do this – I 100 per cent *had* to get a place on that show! Now totally sick of my job, I desperately needed that break.

I had loads of calls from all different people asking me questions, questions and more questions. Then there were lots of meetings – but I still didn't know how far along I had got. I felt it was looking good because they wouldn't leave me alone, but I didn't know for sure.

It was torture because they wouldn't let me tell anyone either. Finally, I was asked in for a meeting and screen test with some of the top producers. I was so nervous that I ended up getting really drunk the night before, and I think I was still drunk when I went to the meeting! They asked me questions on camera and I was really open – probably still the effects of the previous night's alcohol! I thought, I've just got to go for it, really make them laugh and like me, and soon they were laughing their heads off at me and my mad stories.

Then they asked me if I knew anyone else in Essex, and I told them that I knew Joey Essex, who is my first cousin. They were gobsmacked because they had been speaking to Joey as well and had asked him in for a meeting – they had no idea we were related.

I kept on seeing all the *TOWIE* girls in magazines and thinking it could be me after all. I was giddy, knowing I was so close to getting on the show – I just couldn't imagine being in a magazine.

One day, I was asked to do a promotional modelling job at Forever Unique in London's West End. I walked in and there was *TOWIE* star Lucy Mecklenburgh. I had never met her before and she was even more stunning in the flesh. We started chatting and I was desperate to tell her that I was in talks to be in the second series, but I didn't dare because I'd been sworn to secrecy. It was so hard not being able to say anything!

After that, the producers came and did some more filming with me to see what I was like on camera, and I was given the dates when scenes were being filmed, but I still didn't know for sure whether I was on the show. It was mad – I had pinned all my hopes on it but I still hadn't been given confirmation. Me and Joey would call each other to discuss it and see if the other one had heard anything – we both thought we had got it, but we still didn't know for definite. He was the only one I could trust with my secret. We both secretly hoped that we'd be in it together.

A few weeks later, I got a call for filming – it was going to be at Amy Childs' house in Brentwood. Amy had been in the show since the beginning and was one of the girls I'd been looking at on the front of magazines. She ran a beauty salon and was already a massive star of the show. They still hadn't said, 'You've made it on the show' – I only knew I had made it when I was given a contract and started filming! Because it had all been so uncertain whether I would actually make it on to the show, I carried on working for Playboy right up until just a few days before I filmed my first scenes.

When I got to Amy's house, I was asked to act just as I normally would while having a beauty appointment. I hadn't yet met the other cast, so the first time I met them properly was on camera. Obviously, Amy would be there and so would Harry Derbidge and Sam Faiers; I was really nervous. I knew Sam vaguely because she was friends with my brother's girlfriend, but I had never met her properly before.

It was really nerve-wracking and, as I walked in, I was shaking like a leaf. I had to strip off and stand there in a tiny G-string, holding my boobs, while Amy gave me a spray tan!

It's a good job I'm not shy, isn't it? Me and Amy chatted about our boob jobs while she sprayed me. She told me I had great boobs!

So that's how I started in the show. Standing there virtually naked was certainly not your average entrance and I tried to be all confident, but, when I watch that first scene back now, I look like a rabbit caught in the headlights! It was so nerve-wracking and you can tell I'm terrified. I found it really hard to act naturally when the cameras were rolling, and I looked a right state, too. I had just done my make-up the way I would normally but I hadn't realised that TV make-up is so different. You need a lot more to look good on the telly than you do in real life.

I still came out buzzing – I was just so glad I'd got my first scene done.

The next day, it was Joey's turn and we were filming at the King William pub, where I had met the producer the previous year. That scene took ages to film because Joey kept stopping them to ask if he looked OK and how he was meant to smile! He's so insecure about the way he looks. I know people think he puts it on for the cameras but he really doesn't – he's exactly the same in real life, if not even funnier.

Over the next week, I did more scenes: one at the opening of Sam's shop, Minnie's, and one at the Sugar Hut nightclub with Kirk and Mick Norcross. At that point, it was still all top secret until it aired. I had only told a handful of people and it was so strange: here I was filming for a major TV show and yet no one knew about it, and I was living on the money I had saved from Playboy.

I just wanted the first episode to be broadcast so it could finally be out in the open!

Now, nearly 18 months after that first show, my life has changed completely – I never imagined I wouldn't even be able to go to the local shop without being recognised. For the time being, I am happy being in *TOWIE* but I know it won't last forever and I need to make plans for my future. My ambition had always been to be a model, but now I'm 30, I'm too old and so my career aspirations have had to change.

I came from nothing and I've been through a lot to get where I am today. I have experienced so much – some of it good, some of it bad – and I've had a lot of adventures along the way. I've rubbed shoulders with some massive stars and done things that even at the time I've thought, 'This is crazy, what am I doing here?' but that has just made my life all the more exciting.

I've been through some pretty tough times in my life that have led me to where I am today, but I always try to look at the positives when life gets tough. Sometimes I get it wrong because it's hard work, juggling everything – work, being a single mum – and for that reason I try not to have too many regrets. Everything I've done has been to provide a better life for Mady and me.

And everything I've done has shaped who I am now and right now I'm happy with where I'm at. Even though I'm on *The Only Way Is Essex*, I still don't think I've 'made it' – I haven't made so much money that I can retire and I still push my trolley round the supermarket in my tracksuit!

I know the show won't go on forever so I still need to have goals. Fashion is something I've always been passionate about, and I'd love to be a designer, maybe even have my own high-street range.

Over the years, I have done a string of jobs, from flipping burgers in McDonald's to selling double-glazing, and I know now that I couldn't do just anything – it would have to be something I loved. I'm at the age where I won't take any nonsense either. When I was 21, people may have been able to push me about, but not now. I've always wanted to be my own boss and I would love to create my own fashion range and turn it into a proper successful brand.

But overall my dream is the same as most girls – to marry the love of my life, have more kids, work less, be a proper family unit. And live happily ever after.

That's all I've ever really wanted.

Even after everything I have been through, I still believe in that fairytale ending. I've met the man of my dreams – all I need now is my castle to live in.

Those are the things I've wanted ever since I was a little girl – I just didn't realise how much of a rollercoaster my life was going to be before I got there...

CHAPTER TWO

The Early Years

One of my first memories is the day I woke up and realised I was in the house alone.

I was only three years old. One morning, I got out of my bed and went downstairs to get my breakfast. Dad had gone to work – he worked at Billingsgate Market and used to get up at 3am, so I knew he wouldn't be about. I don't remember exactly what happened, but I am guessing I must have gone round the house looking for my dad or next door neighbour Auntie Sylv – she wasn't my real auntie, we just used to call all our neighbours on the estate 'auntie' and 'uncle', but she used to look after me when Dad was at work. I remember going down into the kitchen where our pet dogs were kept in a cage and letting them out.

A few weeks prior to this first memory, my mum had left me with Auntie Sylv and never returned. I cannot really remember what happened, but I know the facts. My mum and dad had split up, and I had stayed on in the house we lived in with my mum. Sylv would often babysit me, and one day Mum dropped me off at hers and never came back to collect me. Poor Auntie Sylv – looking back now, she must have been beside herself with worry, wondering what the hell was going on, but she didn't let on to me. She just looked after me and made me feel safe.

A few days passed and still nothing. My dad came to the house to see me as usual – I think he came to visit at least twice a week – and to his horror no one was home. He knocked at Sylv's to see if she knew anything, and she explained that my mum had disappeared.

My dad immediately moved back into the house and took care of me. Auntie Sylv was always on hand to babysit. Back then Dad used to leave for work at 3am and at first Sylv would come in and get me shortly after and take care of me until he got back. Sylv lived next to us and because it was terraced and the walls so thin, she could hear if anything was going on, plus she had keys.

My memory of the whole thing is really hazy.

Actually, I have so few memories of Mum, too, that I can barely even remember her face. I'll never know why she left and we've never seen her since.

Sometimes it feels like I'm looking down on someone else's life, but actually it's my life. I mean, who does that? What sort of woman just walks out and leaves her child? However bad things get, I don't understand how a mother could do that to her daughter.

I have found it hard being a mum to Mady but, no matter how bad things have got, I would never have walked out and left her. I don't think it will ever sink in what happened that day. Why Mum left me, I guess I'll never know. As far as I'm concerned, I will never meet her.

Things seemed pretty normal when I first came into the world. I was born at King George Hospital in Newbury Park, Essex, on 2 November 1981. My mum and my dad were both very young at the time – she was 19 and he was 20, and I think that has a lot to do with what happened over the next few years.

My dad's best friend had met a girl and asked Dad if he would go on a double date with her and one of her friends – and her friend turned out to be my mum. Apparently, she was wearing a really wacky outfit so maybe I get my unconventional dress sense from her! They hadn't been dating long when Mum fell pregnant. Dad, being the honourable man that he is, asked her to marry him and they had a shotgun wedding.

At the time, my mum, who was originally from Dagenham, was working in an office and my dad had been working at the fish market for a couple of years. Dad was an east London boy, through and through – he had grown up in Bethnal Green but, when he left home, he moved to Essex.

When they married, they got a council house in a place called Clayhall, near Ilford. My mum had been brought up by her nan and granddad, after her own mum and dad left her, and I often wonder if that, too, had something to do with the events of my childhood.

I know I used to see her nan and granddad before my mum left because my family have told me, but I don't remember them. I've met her dad a couple of times, too, and I know he was a hippie, but I don't remember him either. I know very little about her family. In fact, I don't even know if she had any brothers or sisters.

My Nanny Linda – my dad's mum – has a few photo albums with pictures of my mum and dad. There are some from before I was born, including their wedding photos, and others of me when I was a baby, so I know what my mum used to look like. But, honestly, I think, if I hadn't seen those pictures, I wouldn't know what she looked like.

Over the years, my dad has told me a few stories about my mum, and one that sticks in my mind is that Dad was a skinhead at the time and having a skinhead was the height of fashion back then. Anyway, one day my mum decided she wanted to be a skinhead as well and had her head shaved like Britney Spears! Dad tried to point out to her that it was only meant to be the men that shaved their heads, but she was having none of it. I guess she was pretty wacky!

I only really have a few memories of that house in Clayhall – the first one was when I must have been about three. I remember sitting on the stairs, crying because my mum and dad were having a Chinese takeaway and I was meant to be in bed, but I wanted to stay up and try some. Mum had said no, so I was crying because I didn't want to go to bed. Eventually, my dad gave in and let me stay up and have some sweet and sour chicken and a prawn cracker. I was so pleased – I felt really grown up!

I also remember we had two dogs: they were English bull terriers called Brook and Sims, and one of them had had pups, so my dad had put a cage in the kitchen for them. By now Mum had left, and, with Dad out at work, it was just the dogs and me. I don't know how long I sat with them as they jumped round, yelping and barking – I thought it was quite good fun! Our next-door neighbour, Auntie Sylv, heard the commotion from the dogs and, using the spare key she had, let herself in to check that I was OK.

I still had my pyjamas on and I had wet the bed, so I was soaking and stinking of wee. I told Auntie Sylv there was no one at home, just me. She took me back to her house next door and got me cleaned up and washed my pyjamas – I remember them drying on the washing line.

Again, my memory of the exact event is hazy, but, sometime shortly after my dad decided that I should live with Auntie Sylv because of the strange hours he was working. He felt this would give me more stability. So, I moved in with Auntie Sylv, where I stayed for the next nine years. She was just the nicest person you could meet; she was about 20 stone and found it difficult to walk, but nothing was too much trouble.

Her house was always pretty chaotic. Bless her, she didn't have much and material things just didn't matter to her – some of the rooms didn't have carpet, and I remember jumping over the gripper rods so I didn't prick my feet – but she had a heart of gold and she took me on. She looked after me like a daughter and she's an angel inside.

Auntie Sylv became my mum – she was the one who walked me to school, she cooked me my tea and looked after me. My dad was working long hours at the market and he just couldn't care for me on his own, so I lived with Auntie Sylv in the week and then I saw him every weekend.

Auntie Sylv and her husband, Uncle Gordon, already had a 16-year-old daughter called Kelly. They only had a two-bedroom house, so I had to share a room with her. She never complained, and I used to really look up to her. She would be getting ready to go out clubbing with her friends and she would be there, putting on her make-up, listening to music. I would sit for hours watching her transform her face. I think it was those days of watching Kelly that gave me my first taste of make-up and getting dressed up – I used to want to go out with her!

Kelly was really good to me and I loved her like a sister. When she left school, she got a job in McDonald's and she used to bring home the Happy Meal toys for me. They would change the toys every week or so and she would bring me the new one every time. I'd line them up, like they were teddies.

Auntie Sylv was a proper mum – she was a great cook and was always baking cakes. She taught me to bake from an early age. She and Uncle Gordon literally had nothing – there was no carpet in the front room and the electricity meter was always running out.

Gordon was a gardener and plumber and, although they hardly had any money, I never went without. Obviously, my dad used to buy me things and help out, but Auntie Sylv always saved up so she could buy me nice birthday presents. She was so kind.

At Christmas, we used to decorate the tree together and get

really excited. Auntie Sylv ordered things from the catalogue, which she could pay off over the year, so she could treat me. She was so generous and always found the money, somehow. Her house was my home, and I often used to forget that I had actually lived next door because all I could really remember was living with Auntie Sylv.

When I was five, I started at the local school, Parkhill Primary, and the first friend I made was a girl called Sangeeta. Auntie Sylv could never remember her name so she used to call her Leccy Meter, which would really annoy me! Then, just as I was settling in at school, my dad dropped a bombshell: we were going to America.

His dad George – my granddad – lived over there and we were going to stay with him. I had never met my granddad before because he had split with Nanny Linda a long time before that. He had then moved to Chicago and had remarried to a woman called Marilyn. When my dad told me we were going over there for a visit, I was really excited because it would be just the two of us. I was also looking forward to meeting my granddad because, up until then, I hadn't had a proper granddad.

For some reason, I remember the plane journey over there really clearly. The plane seemed massive and the airhostesses were fussing around me, giving me games to play with. I can still picture one game, this box that you could fold out and make into things. My dad and me played with it the whole way to America.

Dad has so much patience – he loves kids and can play games for hours. When the airhostesses kept coming back and forward, bringing us food and drinks, I felt like a princess! I remember getting off the big plane and changing on to a smaller one. I guess there weren't any direct flights to Chicago back then.

Granddad picked us up from the airport in his car and I just lay down across the back seat and pretended to be asleep. It was funny meeting my granddad for the first time. He looked just like my dad – he wasn't a typical granddad at all. Tall and dark, he was handsome and still looked young.

Granddad George and Marilyn lived in a one-bedroom flat, so I slept on a mattress on their bedroom floor and my dad slept on the sofa in the front room. They had a big black dog called Jet, and Marilyn was a really good cook. She cooked spicy foods that I wasn't used to eating at Auntie Sylv's, things like chilli and Caribbean food.

I didn't like sleeping on their floor, though, because I was scared of the dark and used to see shapes – it still freaks me out to this day. One night, my granddad had left a hat over the top of the door and I woke up in the middle of the night and thought there was a man standing there. I screamed the place down and they couldn't calm me, so in the end they let me sleep on the sofa with my dad and I remember feeling really happy. Being with Dad was all I wanted.

We stayed in America for three months – until our money and our visa ran out. It turned out my granddad had told my dad that he could get him a job over there but for some reason it hadn't worked out.

I remember my dad sitting me down and telling me he had to go home and he asked if I wanted to stay. George and

Marilyn had offered to look after me for him because they knew it was tough. But there was no way I was going to be parted from my dad. I didn't want to live in a different country where people spoke in funny voices, so I said I wanted to go home with him.

I was happy with my dad and there was no way I was going to stay without him. I don't remember anything about the flight home but, when we got back, Dad took me to stay with some distant relatives who I had never met before. Auntie Sylv was upset that he had taken me away to America and Dad was worried she'd go mad at him if he took me back. I think he wanted us to stay in America for good, but things didn't work out. When we came back to England, I wanted to go back to Aunty Sylv's, not stay with some random strangers, so I acted up. It worked. I was really naughty and eventually my dad came and got me and took me back to Auntie Sylv.

She was really glad to have me back, but really I just wanted to go with my dad. I worshipped him. To me, he was a superstar – he was good-looking and I honestly believed he could do anything. But, at least when I was at Aunty Sylv's, he was always nearby.

When we came back, I started at a different local school, Gilbert Colvin Primary, and I was always wetting myself – I remember getting changed into dry clothes on several occasions. I made a new friend called Katie Alexander and she soon became my best friend. We were inseparable at school and always sat next to each other.

Katie was the opposite of me – I was blonde and a skinny little thing, but she was dark and sturdy. She had brown hair and freckles, and she was athletic. At the time, I thought she was rich because she lived in Barkingside in a nice area, while I lived on a council estate in Clayhall. We had no carpets, so anything would have seemed posh!

Katie lived in a semi-detached house and she had a garden with a tree in it that we used to climb. I would stay over at her house quite a lot, and I really liked it there. Her mum used to buy Katie little presents and she'd always buy me one too. She had the best sweet cupboard ever! We were allowed to take in a snack bag to have at break time at school and Katie's mum made the best snack bags. It would be a clear sandwich bag, with a drink and chocolates and sweets inside. If I was staying over, she would do a snack bag for me, too, which I loved.

I haven't seen Katie for years – we drifted apart after we left primary school – but I still drive past her old house sometimes now, and it's funny because, all those years ago, I thought it was so big but now it looks small.

My next clear memory is of my sixth birthday because Auntie Sylv organised me a surprise party. She used to go to bingo every week and I would go along with her. Every week, they played the same music in the bingo hall and I used to skip around the chairs while the music played, with Auntie Sylv and all her friends clapping along.

On my sixth birthday, I put on a really pretty dress and Auntie Sylv told me we were going somewhere. We went to a local hall and, when we walked in, all my friends and family were there and the same music from bingo was playing. I skipped in! I was so excited – my Nanny Linda, my dad's mum, was there and lots of the family, as well as people from my class at school.

Auntie Sylv had baked me a huge 'My Little Pony' cake and I loved it. I even had my first kiss at that party with a boy called Ben, who was in my class. I can't remember his surname but I just went up to him and kissed him on the cheek. Even from a young age, I was confident around members of the opposite sex!

It was a really special party and Auntie Sylv had gone to loads of trouble. Even all these years later, I remember everything about it. It is such a special memory.

A few months after my birthday, I went to school as normal – I used to walk there by myself, even though I was only six – and, when I got there, I realised that Katie wasn't in that day. I'd already swapped my lunch tokens but I decided I didn't want to be at school without her so I just left again and walked back home, without saying a word to anyone.

I told Auntie Sylv that school wasn't on that day and she believed me. So we caught the bus into Debden and went shopping for what she called 'goodies'. We were gone all day. Then on the way back, I needed the toilet, so I ran from the bus stop back home to go for a wee. Auntie Sylv could only shuffle slowly so I ran ahead, and, when I got back, there were loads of people waiting and they said the police had been called because I had disappeared from school.

By the time I heard Auntie Sylv shuffling up the path, I knew I was in big trouble. She was absolutely fuming! They had been trying to contact her and everyone was really worried.

They'd even had the police helicopter out looking for me! The police came to talk to me and told me that I had caused a lot of trouble and, when I went back into school the next day, the headmaster shouted at me.

Auntie Sylv didn't stay angry for long, and the whole thing was soon forgotten and everything went back to normal, but I never did it again.

All my memories of living at Auntie Sylv's are happy ones – even though they were poor, they always treated me. Auntie Sylv didn't have any of her own money really because she didn't work and Uncle Gordon only gave her a bit each week so she had to save up for anything she wanted. My dad used to give her money every week for me, though.

Uncle Gordon used to go to the pub after work and then he'd come back and would always sit in the same chair to watch the telly. When he got up, Auntie Sylv used to whisper to me to check down the sides of the chair to see if any coins had fallen out of his pockets. It was our secret way of getting a few extra quid for treats.

Sometimes Uncle Gordon would take me to the pub with him and buy me a fizzy drink, which I always thought was a real treat. Auntie Sylv was always so good to me but, looking back, I was a bit of a naughty child and didn't do what I was told. She must have been tearing her hair out. Every night, I used to play out with the other kids from the estate and I would never come home when I was supposed to.

I got to learn pretty quickly that Auntie Sylv couldn't walk very fast, so, when she came out to get me to come in, I would just run away from her. Even when she was shouting at me from across the street, I tried to delay going home for as long as possible.

Every house had a big concrete doorstep and I remember Auntie Sylv would give me a packet of chalks and let me colour in the doorstep to keep me busy and out of trouble. I loved doing that.

When I look back, I had a lovely childhood – I knew everyone on the estate and everyone was friendly. There was a shop in the middle and I used to run errands for Auntie Sylv when she needed things. Every summer, me and all the other kids would literally spend the whole six weeks outdoors; we were probably a nightmare for the neighbours but we had great fun. We knew where everyone lived and we got to know who was miserable. We used to torment them by playing 'Knock Down Ginger' (where you knock on a door, then run off and hide) for hours on end. We would also have water fights and play for hours, getting totally soaked, and other days we would have street parties on the green near our house.

When I was a bit older, Auntie Sylv got a job working at the bingo so she had a bit more money and I remember when we finally got carpet in the front room. I reckon it was about five years after I moved in, and it was a big deal. Other people took things like carpet for granted, but I still remember the feel of it under my feet. It was so nice and warm after the cold bare floors we had before!

At weekends, Dad would come and take me out and then we'd go back to his house in – I liked it there because it was just him and me. I also saw him on a Tuesday after school, when he would pick me up and take me to swimming lessons and, later, karate lessons, and then to McDonald's for tea. I loved spending time with my dad. Often, instead of going to his house, we'd go to visit the rest of his family.

There was my dad's mum, Nanny Linda, who lived nearby in Essex, and also his gran, Nanny Daisy, who was really my great-gran and lived in east London.

Nanny Daisy was always the head of the family. She was brilliant. A real matriarch, she kept the family together. Everyone would pile into her flat whenever there was a drama – I've never met anyone so caring as my Nanny Daisy.

We all used to go and get pie and mash from a shop called Kelly's on the Roman Road near her flat and then take it back there to eat it. She had this silver cutlery we had to eat with and, because it was so old, all the silver was coming off and it used to leave a horrible taste in your mouth. Nanny Daisy died five years ago at the age of 99 and she was an amazing lady. Although she was little and frail with curly grey hair, she was a really strong woman.

Nanny Daisy was a proper old-fashioned East Ender and had a real Cockney accent, like you hear on films. She loved kids, and she always loved having us round. She always had loads of sweets and treats, which for some bizarre reason she used to keep in the freezer. The chocolate buttons would be rock-hard and we'd be nearly breaking our teeth on the boiled sweets!

Although she didn't have loads of money, she was always giving us cash and telling us to go and treat ourselves. When I was younger, she used to give me £20 and tell me to go and buy some clothes and then come back and give her a fashion show. I'd go into her bedroom – she lived in a one-bedroom flat – and try it all on and then model it for her. She'd go: 'Oooh, that's nice! How much was that?' And then she'd go on about what a bargain it was.

Nanny Linda is great too, just like her mum. We are really close and I still speak to her nearly every day. The relationship I have with Nanny Linda now is what I imagine you'd have with a mum: if she annoys me, I can tell her I'm pissed off (and vice versa). When I was younger, she always wore really strong perfume and big shoulder pads! I suppose it was the eighties, so that was the fashion back then.

She is one of those people who can't stop feeding you – as soon as you walk in the door, she's got a meal prepared and is trying to feed you up. She always buys the food she knows you like and her house is really cosy. If ever I'm upset, I go to my Nanny Linda's because it feels like home. She's lived in the same house since I was a little girl and it is always so welcoming. Mady loves going round there because she always buys her sweets and there's this big toy box there, so she's got loads of things to play with.

A lot of people think maybe she should have let me and my dad live with her after Mum left. But Nanny Linda had just brought up her own kids and she'd had a hard life and she said no. I don't resent her for that at all. Maybe life would have turned out differently... I'll never know.

Then there was my dad's sister, Auntie Tina, and her husband, Uncle Donald, who lived in Bermondsey, south London. I loved Auntie Tina – she always looked glamorous and smelled of perfume. I think, when my mum left, she wanted me to go and live with her but she was only young and didn't have kids of her own yet, and my dad felt it wasn't fair on her because she should enjoy being young while she could.

She always made me feel really welcome and I loved being at her house. Uncle Donald used to drive over to collect me and I'd look forward to seeing them both. When I was five, Auntie Tina told me she was having a baby and I was really excited. I helped her get the nursery all ready and I just could not wait for that baby to be born. I used to sit in the nursery and think, 'Wow, soon there will be a little baby in here, a cousin for me!'

Her pregnancy seemed to last for ages but eventually the baby came. She had a little girl and called her Francesca – Frankie – and I was over the moon she was a girl!

As much as I loved Auntie Sylv, I still never wanted to go back there after my weekends with my family and, as I grew older, I realised that my lot were quite different from Auntie Sylv and her family.

Auntie Sylv had a heart of gold and was very loving, but she never cared about material things or the way she looked. She only had one pair of shoes and, as welcoming and homely as it was, her house was far from immaculate. She really wasn't bothered about appearances or airs and graces, but she was the salt of the earth – decent, hardworking and kind – and I can never put into words how grateful I am for what she did for me when I was a little girl. And Gordon and Kelly, too – I will always love them and have so many fond and happy memories of being there.

Over the years, Auntie Sylv was so loving towards me – she

put up with all kinds. I used to wet the bed but she never complained; she would just clean me up and wash the sheets, never passing comment. She was such a great mother figure to me that I never even thought about my own mum, and she wasn't spoken about either. Auntie Tina told me that I once told her that I lived with Auntie Sylv because my mummy didn't love me, but I don't remember saying it. I guess to other people it was a difficult start in life but I can honestly say that I was really happy as a child. I had a lovely childhood, thanks to Auntie Sylv and my dad and his family.

Social workers used to come and visit me once a fortnight to check that my living arrangements were going well; they would sit me down on my own and ask me questions about Auntie Sylv and Uncle Gordon and if I was happy. They used to record everything I said on a Dictaphone and then, after they had finished talking to me, they would let me play with it while they went to speak to Auntie Sylv in private.

It was only when I was a bit older that I really got to know all my family. They had fancy clothes, sleek and glossy hair and always smelled nice. And I was definitely more like them. I remember when I was about seven I refused to wear anything but party shoes! I was a proper princess. Obviously, the party shoes I wore weren't meant to be worn all the time and weren't hard wearing, so I was getting through a pair every few weeks and my family kept having to buy me new ones.

It was around that time that my dad met a woman called Karen and they started dating. I liked her straight away. She was a model and I thought she was beautiful. Back then, she looked like a brunette Claudia Schiffer and, together, she and my dad made a very glamorous pair. They were like something out of a film – a real Hollywood couple!

After a while, they moved in together to a one-bedroom flat in east London. It was small, and at the time Karen worked full-time in a bank, so it wasn't practical for me to go and live with them. Then, when I was 11, Karen fell pregnant and had a little boy – my brother– and all my dreams came true.

Ever since I could remember, I had wanted to live with my dad and, finally, that wish became a reality.

CHAPTER THREE

A Proper Family

When Karen was pregnant, I remember panicking that it would be a baby girl and I would be the ugly one because, with those two as parents, she would bound to be gorgeous. My dad must have picked up on those fears about the new baby because I remember him telling me, 'Don't worry about the new baby. I'll always love you.'

Anyway, when my brother was born, my dad was more settled and felt more sorted in life with a new house and things, so he decided it was best I move in with him. I know it was his plan all along, but he didn't want to uproot me until he knew 100 per cent – which he did as this point.

With my dad, Karen and a new baby, living in a one-bedroom flat wasn't going to be easy. I think Auntie Sylv was really sad to see me go but she was doing it in my best interests. That's the kind of person she is – even though it broke her heart, she was doing it for me.

My dad managed to scrape enough money together to get a house in Beckton, east London, which was a cheap area and the only place they could afford. He literally spent every penny buying the house so we could be a proper family. I had my own bedroom, which was in the loft – right up in the eaves – and he took hours painstakingly decorating it and making it perfect for me. In my room, I had a double bed and a telly. I had finally got my dream – living with Dad and being with my new family.

Auntie Sylv helped me pack up all my things. She was a proper hoarder and never threw anything away so I had loads and loads of stuff that I had accumulated over the years. We put it all in bin bags and that's how I turned up at this new house with my stuff – most of which was only fit for the bin, anyway! The thing was, I wouldn't throw any of it away because that was how Auntie Sylv had brought me up. God knows what Karen must have thought when I rocked up with all that junk.

Despite having my dream come true, I wasn't happy. My dad was working every hour to pay for this house that they couldn't really afford. Karen went back to work full-time at the bank and my brother went to nursery. We had moved over the six-week summer holiday and I was due to start secondary school in the September.

I went to Brampton Manor in Newham and, when I started there, I hated it – I was different to all the other east London kids and I didn't fit in. There was a much wider ethnic mix at the new school and I wasn't used to it. It was really hard and took a while, but eventually I settled in and managed to make loads of new friends.

Finally, I was happy – I had a nice home, I liked school and my step-mum Karen was really good to me. Most of all, I loved my baby brother. I'd already looked after baby Frankie all those years before with Auntie Tina and I loved babies. I just wanted to mother him and I used to help Karen feed him and change his nappies. It was like having a real-life baby doll!

When I was 13, and totally settled at my new school with all my new friends, my dad announced that we were moving again. He had bought a run-down house back in Essex to renovate so we could afford to be back in an area where he wanted to be. Plus, Karen had had two more kids by then – my sisters Frances and Demi – and we needed more space. Also, I don't think they approved of my East End 'ghetto' friends and wanted to move me back to Essex.

By this time, I didn't want to go back – I was gutted about leaving all my new mates. But my dad told me he had bought this house in Collier Row, near Romford, and we were moving, and I was going to start all over again at a posh school called Bower Park. I remember he showed me the brochure for the school and then I really didn't want to go there.

At Brampton Manor, we could pretty much wear what we wanted within reason, the uniform was not strict at all, but in this brochure all the girls were wearing blazers and ties and looked totally different from me and all my friends. They looked so posh and stuffy! How was I going to fit in there?

My dad and Karen had made their decision, though, and that was that. We moved just before the end of the summer term, and all through the summer holiday I was going backwards and forwards to Beckton to meet up with my old friends. I also used to stay a lot with my cousins, Frankie and Joey, in Bermondsey, south London, as well.

When the start of the new term came around, I couldn't believe how big the school was – it was massive compared to my old one. There I was in a blazer that was several sizes too big for me, looking like a right idiot. And I had the shock of my life when I saw that none of the girls looked anything like the ones in the brochure.

Those girls had all been wearing knee-length skirts but in real life they were wearing mini-skirts and had make-up on and tight shirts showing off their boobs! It was my first taste of what Essex girls looked like.

On the first day, they asked a girl called Helen Woolf to show me around. She was really pretty and looked so cool and, although she was shy, she was very popular. I soon realised that all the girls were a lot more grown up than me. They were reading teenage magazines like *Mizz*, and on Saturdays they used to go shopping for music, which was something me and my old friends had never done. There was me thinking I was the cool one from east London, but really I was a tomboy compared to all these girls.

I quickly realised I had to change the way I looked but my dad wouldn't let me wear short skirts or put on make-up. That's when I got in the habit of putting on my make-up and hitching my skirt up as far as I could on the way to school, and then I would rub it all off on the way home and roll down my skirt. I'd be asking Helen if every trace of make-up was gone to make sure I didn't get told off.

Then the bullying started. First of all, it was just name-calling – they used to tell me I looked like I had Down's Syndrome and I looked like an alien. Unfortunately, their first impression of me was that I was ugly and it stuck: you're so impressionable and sensitive at that age and kids can be so cruel. They used to sing 'Spaceman' at me, a song in the charts around that time, and they would write it all over my books. It was so different from my old school in Beckton.

One day, it was particularly bad – a boy in my class called Lee Hayton tried to set fire to my hair with a lighter. The other kids would be making fun of me and I'd sit there with tears streaming down my face, but they just carried on. I was in floods of tears every single day.

On another particularly bad day, something terrible happened – and, to this day, it is still one of the most embarrassing things that has ever happened to me. We were doing PE, as usual, and no one ever wore the regulation PE kit, which was basically a big pair of black granny knickers – instead, they used to wear black cycling shorts. For some reason, I had decided to wear white cycling shorts, and at the end of the lesson I realised I had come on my period in the middle of the class. There was a small leakage in the crotch of my shorts so I just stuffed them in the top of my bag to sort out later.

Next thing, we were in a French class and one of the boys – I can't remember his name – got a metal metre ruler out, leaned over and fished my shorts out of the bag. Because I had taken them off in a hurry, they were inside out and when he flicked them on the floor they landed with the bloodstain in full view of the class. Everyone saw the blood and the whole class started shouting, 'Eurgh, that's disgusting!' and making vomiting noises.

I just put my head down on the desk and started crying. Everyone was tormenting me and yet the teacher said nothing. I was so mortified. The next thing was everyone in my class told everyone else, and within hours it went round the whole school. What was even worse was the fact that the story was obviously embellished along the way, as kids do, and the cycling shorts became a pair of lace knickers that were now 'covered' in blood.

What happened haunted me for months – even to this day it's one of the most embarrassing moments of my life.

Through all this, Helen and I became the best of friends and soon we were inseparable. She is still one of my best friends today. I really looked up to her at the beginning and even tried to cut my hair like her because she fitted in and I didn't. Eventually, I stopped caring about the bullies because I had Helen, who was cool and popular.

When the bullies eventually realised I wasn't bothered any more, they stopped doing it quite so much. Helen was my rock – she was good-looking but shy, whereas I was more confident and we made a good team. We used to stay at each other's house all the time and our likes and dislikes became the same: we were both into clothes and make-up, and used to dress the same.

I was never any good at school – I just wasn't interested. I cared more about false eyelashes and fake tan. I had a problem with authority and I didn't care about academic qualifications. I'd decided I wanted to be a model so I wasn't bothered about exams. It was ironic – I'd gone from being a nerd and being called ugly to wanting to become a model. I was determined to prove them all wrong.

I told my dad I wanted to be a model and kept asking him if I could enter modelling competitions but he always said no. Then, when I was 15, there was an advert in the *Romford Recorder* for a modelling competition organised by the newspaper. My dad told me I could enter and I was over the moon. I had my pictures taken and the photographer told me I had potential. The results were based on a public vote and, of course, no one voted for me because we didn't really have any friends or family who read the *Romford Recorder*.

However, as well as being told I had potential, they later used my picture on the front page of the *Romford Recorder* to advertise the modelling competition. That was it for me: I'd had a taste of it and now I had real ambition. I was far more interested in becoming a model than in being at school, and I never tried very hard in my lessons after that.

It was also around this time that I discovered boys and there were two lads in my year at school that everyone fancied – Danny Sawkins and Danny Emberson. Danny Sawkins was the fittest in the school; he looked like a young Ben Affleck. Literally, the whole school was after him and I tried to ask him out, but he wouldn't go out with me. He called me a fuck-up!

Danny Emberson, on the other hand, was more of a bad guy. Me and my best friend, Helen, started hanging around with him and a few of his friends. I really liked him, we got on well, and we used to hang around together all time. We were too young to get into any pubs or anything, so we used to just hang around the streets – we called it street raking – and me and Danny would always chat.

I guess, looking back, it was flirting but I didn't have a clue back then! We went on like that for ages and eventually he asked me out, but it took a long time to get to the boyfriend and girlfriend stage.

I think in the beginning he was embarrassed because of all the names I got called – I don't think he wanted everyone to know we were together, but eventually he made it official. When he said, 'Will you be my girlfriend?' I thought it was the best thing ever! I couldn't believe it – I was the one everyone had called ugly and now I was going out with one of the most popular blokes in the school.

As soon as we started dating, the bullying completely stopped – he went round to all the people who had ever been nasty to me and threatened them! Me and Danny soon became inseparable. He had long hair and everyone thought he was really cool. But he smoked, which I didn't like. My family were really anti-smoking, and my dad didn't approve and never seemed to like Danny. I'm not sure why but I guess it's because he was my first boyfriend. Plus, I don't think Dad would have liked anyone I went out with! I guess that's a dad's job. He was just being protective of his little girl – no man was good enough – plus, he didn't like the fact that Danny hung around on street corners. Only now, as a mum myself, I understand him; I wouldn't want that for my girl either.

We dated for a year and we literally spent all our time together – he was my first love. On my 16th birthday, he bought me a ring and everything; I proper loved him. I would have married him, which looking back now is hilarious!

After we had been together a while, we slept together – he was my first – and I fell even more in love.

I thought everything was perfect – his mum and dad were really nice and always made me feel welcome at their house and Danny was the love of my life – but, while our relationship was amazing, my schoolwork was going downhill fast.

I started dressing up, always had fake nails on and wore false eyelashes, mini-skirts and heels. I didn't care about school at all – in fact, I hated all the teachers and I bunked off a few times with a big gang of people. Because there were so many of us missing, we always seemed to get caught!

One day, a few of us had decided to skive off early and I went back to my friend Claire's house. She lived not far from the school and her mum was out at work so we didn't think we'd get caught. Unfortunately, the school had phoned her mum at work and told her Claire wasn't there, so she rang home and started shouting at her. I was petrified she would tell my dad, who I knew would be absolutely furious, so we came up with a plan: we put a boiling-hot flannel on Claire's forehead and she lay down on the couch.

When her mum got home, we pretended that Claire had been feeling sick and dizzy, and I had helped her home because

I didn't want to let her go on her own. We didn't really think we'd get away with it, but her mum fell for it! We must have been pretty convincing because she totally swallowed it. She told me that, if my dad said anything, she would speak to him and tell him what had happened.

I knew he would see through it straight away if I told him, but he was much more likely to believe another adult. So I went home and Dad was furious. I was shitting myself all the way home because I didn't think he'd fall for our story, and I was dreading what would happen as soon as I opened the front door. The next thing, he yelled, 'You are in big trouble, young lady! You're grounded.'

Being grounded was the worst thing ever – my dad was really strict and he was always grounding me and I hated it. It didn't just mean I wasn't allowed out, it also meant that I wasn't allowed any contact with the outside world. I was banned from using the phone and he even used to take my telly out of my room. It was like torture – I used to sit and watch the buses go past because there was nothing else to do.

Anyway, on that day, I was determined not to get grounded so I told him my made-up story about Claire being ill, but he was having none of it. I said, if he didn't believe me, he could ring Claire's mum. I thought he'd say no and just ground me anyway, but he went off and rang her. She said I had been really kind, helping Claire home when she wasn't feeling well. I couldn't believe my luck – I'd got out of it!

So there I am all happy because I've been let off when my best friend Helen walked past my house, looking really miserable. I ran outside and asked her where she was going and she said she was running away! Her mum had found out she'd bunked off too, but she'd gone and grounded her.

I was so pleased I'd been let off that I hadn't given a thought to anyone else. Anyway, the next thing, Helen's mum – who was a primary-school teacher and quite well-to-do – came driving past and pulled up alongside Helen and told her not to be silly and to get in the car. She was saying, 'Please, Helen, come on, get in the car and we can talk about this.' It was so funny; she was saying it all posh and politely, totally different to my family. If that had been my dad, he'd have got out of the car and dragged me in!

It looked so funny – her mum saying, 'Please, Helen, just get in the car,' and Helen saying, 'No, I'm running away,' even though she didn't have a bag or anything with her – that I couldn't stop laughing.

People had started staring by this point and Helen's mum didn't like to make a scene, so eventually she said that, if Helen got in the car, she would un-ground her, and Helen was over the moon. We'd both got away with it!

I could tell Helen's mum was none too impressed, but she still liked me because Helen and me were so close.

Although I never really bothered in class and was always being told to try harder, I didn't go out of my way to get into trouble – things just seemed to happen to me! One day, I had got in late so I had to walk in via the office to tell them why I was late. Anyway, the ladies in the office told me to take off my false eyelashes and I said no. They kept saying it, but I was having none of it – I told them they couldn't make me, I made such a fuss. I remember saying, 'You can't tell me what to do – you're not even teachers, you just work in the office!' Then – cocky little cow that I was – I told them that it was an infringement of my human rights!

They were none too impressed, so they went to fetch the headmaster and one of them told him that I'd been really insulting and called her a goat! Now I'm not saying I was in the right, but I definitely hadn't called her a goat. There was no way I would have used the word 'goat'. I was only 15 – I'd have said 'bitch', not 'goat'!

Anyway, the headmaster hauled me into his office and shouted at me. He was so angry the spit was coming out of his mouth as he was shouting! I told him, if I had wanted to offend her, I wouldn't have said 'goat', but that just made him more angry because I wouldn't admit to it.

He told me to write down exactly what I had said, so I did. But, when I took it back to him, he wasn't happy and tore it up and told me to do it again. I ended up doing it three times, but he still wasn't happy because I hadn't admitted to calling the secretary a goat.

I kept trying to say I hadn't said it, but they wouldn't believe me. The secretary obviously made it up to get me in trouble. The headmaster was so furious he rang my dad, and Dad and my step-mum Karen came up to the school. They sat them down and told them what had happened. Dad was livid and grounded me for a month. All over my false eyelashes!

From then on, every time I did any little thing wrong, the headmaster would get straight on the phone to my dad and I'd be grounded. It was awful! The older I got, the less I cared about schoolwork, though – I was more bothered about going out and having a laugh with my mates.

All through my last year at school, I was going for more modelling shoots and entering competitions, and I was even more determined that modelling was what I wanted to do. By the time I did my GCSEs, I had literally given up and failed all my exams except art. And I only passed that because I found some old art work of my dad's and handed that in for my assessment. They were really old-fashioned pictures of bodybuilders and singer Kate Bush! I can't believe they actually thought it was my work.

Around this time, I started hearing rumours that Danny had been seeing another girl behind my back. We'd been together nearly a year by this point and, when people started telling me that this girl Tracey was going round boasting that she'd stayed over at his house, I was livid. I confronted Danny, but he denied it and I couldn't find any proof, so I decided that I would have it out with Tracey.

I found out where she was going to be one day and I marched down there and gave her a slap! I wasn't going to have her going around saying she'd been with my boyfriend.

Over the time that Danny and me had been together, I had started hanging around with some older friends and going to pubs. I was desperate to go to clubs and wanted to go out drinking. Meanwhile, Danny was still quite happy hanging around the streets smoking. I didn't want that – I wanted to get all dressed up and go out, and I guess I outgrew him.

A few weeks after I slapped Tracey, Danny dumped me for

another girl. She was a traveller and I can't remember her name. I was a bit gutted but it was more that my pride had been dented because he'd dumped me than that I actually cared.

I had been head over heels for him a year earlier when he'd seemed so cool but now I'd realised that, actually, he wasn't all that. I guess he wasn't the love of my life after all. When he dumped me, I'd already been flirting with a few guys I'd met on nights out anyway, so I suppose I wasn't bothered for long.

Shortly after we split, he ended up going out with Tracey – the one who claimed she was seeing him behind my back. They later got married and had kids, and they are still together now. I still don't know if he did cheat on me with her, though.

The time came to leave school and I needed to find a job. While I was at school, I'd had a Saturday job working in a card shop, where I got paid £15 a day, which is shocking by today's standards and, even back then, it was a pittance. It all went on toiletries – I used to go straight to Boots and spend the lot on make-up and beauty stuff.

By the time I was 16, I wanted more money for going out – although my dad wouldn't let me go clubbing – so I left the card shop. I asked Kelly – Auntie Sylv's daughter – to get me a job in McDonald's because the pay was better.

Even though the pay was much better – I used to get £60 a fortnight – I hated it, so I quit and just walked out without telling them I was leaving. That was what I did with pretty much every job I've ever had – I've never been one to stick at something I hate for long, if I can help it.

Next came a stint working in telesales, selling double-glazing, but I was useless at it. Some friends from school worked there as well. We were on a really rubbish basic wage and then we'd get commission if we sold anything, but I never did. We used to go down the list and find the people with the funniest names and then we'd phone and ask to speak to them, and just crack up laughing.

It's no wonder I didn't sell anything!

Anyway, after I quit the telesales job, I really didn't know what to do next. My dad wasn't happy because I didn't have a job and he didn't want to see me wasting my life. He was also worried about the group of friends I had because some of them smoked cannabis and took other drugs. I guess maybe he thought they would be a bad influence, but I had no interest in taking drugs.

Then Dad was offered a job for 2 years over in Majorca. The job was well paid, so as a family we relocated there. My dad organised a job for me before he went, which was working for a company that organised bar crawls.

Things were looking up again. Just a month after leaving school and still only 16, I headed over to Majorca to start a new life in the sun.

CHAPTER FOUR

Growing Up

I can seriously say that I had the time of my life in the Balearic Islands. It was 1998 and I was young, single and up for partying every night.

The job my dad's friend got me was selling tickets for the bar crawls in a famous party resort. It was pretty straightforward – I had to go around in the daytime getting groups of holidaymakers to sign up to the bar crawls in the evenings. They would have to give half the money up front and then pay the rest later.

Me, my dad, Karen and the kids had been to the resort before on holiday, so it wasn't like it was totally unknown, plus I had people looking out for me so it wasn't as daunting as it might sound. It was certainly a different experience to our last family holiday there. I hadn't really seen the craziness of it all – the infamous strip of bars, all built on top of each other, some high up and reached by many winding steps, and even more bars built deep underground. There were enough bars and clubs to keep even the most hardcore party people going all night.

I was still only 16, but I'd grown into my looks and was much more confident in myself. I knew I was prettier and I'd started getting more male attention. This probably made the job easier, if I'm honest, but I was really good at it and it paid well, too.

Back then, the cost of living was so cheap out there – I'd never had so much available cash to go out and enjoy myself. The company running the bar crawls treated us well. They gave me a moped and I even had a mobile phone when they were just starting out and hardly anyone else had one. I had money in my pocket, I'd made loads of friends and life was good.

I moved into an apartment, which I shared with twin girls – Suzy and Sarah from Manchester – and two boys, one from Birmingham and the other from Newcastle. It was a bit cramped with all of us there, but, with the work during the daytime and being out all night partying, it didn't seem important and just seemed to add to the fun.

Suzy and Sarah were great fun – they worked with me selling tickets for the bar crawls. We had loads of laughs, although we did manage to end up in trouble from time to time. On one occasion, Suzy and I had been working together during the day, selling tickets as usual, and had spotted a group of about 20 German tourists. We decided to do whatever we could to sell them tickets because a sale that big would make us a load of commission (we didn't usually see groups of quite so many lads, so we made it our mission to convince them to buy tickets). Suzy promised them that, as they'd spent so much with us, we'd drop off a crate of wine at their hotel later that afternoon.

Later that day, I said, 'So, when are we sorting out this wine for the Germans, then?'

Suzy just laughed and said, 'We're not.'

'*What*? I don't understand,' I said.

She replied, 'I only said that so they'd buy tickets – I didn't mean it.'

It turned out to be a total lie – she'd never intended to buy it at all. I was so naive I thought she had planned a nice gesture! But her point was that they were tourists who would only be there for a week or so and we'd never see them again. That's how it was among many of the workers – they would all target the palest of holidaymakers, as this would signify the ones who'd just arrived and were easier to blag!

That same evening, Suzy was off out with her boyfriend, so it was just Sarah and me who went out together. We were outside a bar at the top of the strip when the Germans from earlier that day spotted us and came marching over. Now Suzy and Sarah were identical twins, so clearly they had mistaken one for the other and started having a go at Sarah, who didn't have a clue what was going on. She had a big German guy in her face, shouting, 'Where is my wine?' and she just looked totally confused. I wasn't having him speaking to Sarah like that when it wasn't anything to do with her, so I tried to explain that it wasn't her, it was her twin sister, but he wasn't listening or thought we were lying.

As he got angrier, he started getting right in her face and was being really aggressive, so I kept shouting that he was wrong and it wasn't her. Next thing I knew, he turned round and gave me a great big slap round my face! I couldn't believe it.

Now, in the resort, the rules were strict: workers stuck together and any trouble from tourists was not tolerated, which could end really badly for some poor drunken soul on holiday getting rowdy, not realising that suddenly he had the entire strip's worth of workers to answer to! Sarah and Suzy were well known in the resort: they'd worked on ticket selling for a while and, well, they were identical twins and both quite loud so not easily missed.

On this particular night, our exchange with the German tourists was spotted by one of the doormen at a nightclub, just across from where we were standing and he quickly came running over. A fight broke out between the doorman and the Germans. More people got involved and then it all spiralled out of control! I knew they were just sticking up for me – which was fair enough, because he had hit a girl – but I didn't expect it all to kick off like that.

The fight ended up going all the way down the whole of the strip as more and more people got involved. It was a proper street brawl and all because Suzy, who wasn't even there, and I had managed to start it. What a nightmare!

Later on that year, I went back to England for a two-week holiday to see my family and met up with all my old friends. It was great to catch up with everyone and we went on a night out together to a place called Country Club in Abridge. It was my favourite place to go clubbing and I'd always be up on the stage, dancing the night away. While I was dancing, I spotted a guy at the bar who was really fit – I remember turning to my friend Helen and saying, 'See that guy over there? He's gorgeous!'

A bit later, we got chatting and he asked me what I did for a living, and I told him I was a model, even though I wasn't. Modelling was still what I wanted to do when I'd finished having fun out in Majorca. I asked what he did and he told me he was a footballer. His name was Danny Chapman and he played for Barnet FC. He was 19 and from Bethnal Green in east London. It turned out that he lived near my Nanny Daisy. I really fancied him, so, when he said, 'Can I have your number?', I said yes straight away.

He rang me the next day and said he wanted to meet me, and he drove all the way from east London to Collier Row to pick me up. We drove around in his car for a bit and chatted loads. I liked him a lot – he was good-looking and funny, plus I really fancied him.

From then on, we were inseparable and I spent the rest of my holiday with him. During this time, he took me to meet his parents, we slept together and everything was amazing; I was head over heels. I had all these visions of him being a successful footballer and me being a successful model, but I was only home for two weeks and I had to go back to Majorca. I wanted to stay in England but I had my job over there, which I liked and made me good money; I was gutted.

I was totally torn between staying with Danny and going

back, but eventually I decided to return to the Balearic Islands. I told him I'd come back for him if he just waited a few months for me and he said he would. As far as I was concerned, this was true love.

When I went back to Majorca, I thought about Danny all the time and I cried over him every night for three months. At the beginning, I would phone him as often as I could and we'd talk for hours. But I loved my job and I had loads of friends, I was having a fantastic time and gradually I settled into my life in Majorca more and more.

Three months on, just before I was due to go home, I met someone else. Lee was 24, so he seemed really mature. He drove a convertible Golf and he was the top ticket seller in the whole resort, a real highflier in the workers' community! I set my sights on him. I was determined I would make him mine, and I did.

Before I could make a move on Lee, I had to finish with Danny, so I rang him and told him I wasn't coming home. He was furious.

I remember saying, 'Danny, I've got something to tell you. I've changed my mind. I'm not coming back.'

He yelled back, 'I don't believe this! I've waited three months for you and now you're not coming. And I'd bought you a really nice present as well.'

It turns out he'd bought me a diamond bracelet that he was going to give me when I got back and he was fuming with me. All that time, he'd been waiting for me and there I was, telling him I wasn't coming back! He'd told all the players in his football team that he'd bought me this bracelet and I think that's why he was more pissed off – I'd made him look a fool in front of his mates.

He was shouting at me down the phone and then he yelled, 'Don't ever let me see you around Bethnal Green again, or I'll slap you!' before slamming the phone down.

Me and Lee got together after I finished with Danny, and after a couple of months things became quite serious between us. Living with four other people was starting to annoy me – the flat was always a complete tip – and Lee had his own place.

I used to spend most nights over at his place and, although the sex wasn't great, I liked the fact that he was a big deal over there. It may have just been Majorca but he had status and money. I realised that the problem was that I didn't really fancy him – not like Danny – but I put it to the back of my mind.

One night, me and Lee went out for a few drinks at one of the bars on the strip. We didn't really go out to the strip that often; the novelty of all these bars on your doorstep had worn off and we were a couple so we used to stay in more. This seemingly innocent drink was to create a whole new nightmare, which would make the fight with the German tourists pale into insignificance.

After a few early drinks, we moved on to a nightclub. Anyone who's ever been to Majorca will most likely have fond memories of the clubs on the main strips; they are great institutions. Unfortunately, the club we went to was upstairs, meaning some tricky negotiation of the many steps on the way out in the early hours! After a couple more drinks in the nightclub, we decided to call it a night.

We were leaving the club when the DJ played Whitney Houston's 'It's Not Right But It's Okay', which at the time was 'my song'. Over the years, I've had several tunes that I just love and play over and over again. This was my current favourite, so I told Lee to hang on and ran back inside the club. Just as I got on to the dancefloor, a fight must have broken out – although I didn't see it – and someone threw a bottle at someone else and it smashed and showered me with broken glass.

It all happened so quickly. I didn't know what had gone on and I didn't know I was hurt until I looked down and saw my arm was bleeding. I must have been in shock. Then I felt something on my forehead and realised my head was also cut. It seemed like slow motion to begin with, and then the next thing there was blood everywhere – it was pouring down my face. I ran out of the club, down the stairs and into the middle of the road below. I was screaming because I didn't know what had happened and all I could see was this blood. At the best of times, I'm terrible at the sight of blood and I went into meltdown. I didn't know where the blood was coming from at this point – I was standing in the street, going mental.

Lee found me out on the strip and managed to call a first aider from one of the other bars, who came straight over. They took me back to Lee's place and tried to calm me down. I was taken to hospital, where I had an X-ray, a tetanus jab and got stitched up. The cut actually wasn't that big, but it was right in the middle of my eyebrows and, when I saw it in the mirror, I couldn't stop crying.

My dream had always been modelling but now I had a big

scar right in the middle of my face! I cried for hours – I was absolutely devastated and thought my modelling career was over before it had even begun. I was sure any chance of doing modelling would be out of the window. I had a big, ugly, red scar on my face and I was so gutted. I had to wear butterfly stitches on it for ages and, for years afterwards, it was red and really noticeable.

For ages, after that horrible night, I would sit and stare at myself in the mirror, wishing the scar would just disappear. If only I hadn't run back in that club to dance, it would never have happened. I was in the wrong place at the wrong time and because of that the rest of my life might be affected and my dreams shattered.

The scar has faded a lot now but you can still see it if I don't cover it up with make-up. Now it's just part of my face because it has been there for so long, but at the time it was a huge deal to me and I was devastated.

Things with Lee plodded on, and after a while I talked him into getting an apartment with me, so I was finally able to leave my mates in the shared apartment. Me and Lee lived together for eight months and things were pretty good between us, although I still didn't really fancy him. I had started to get homesick – I missed my dad, my brother, my sisters and all my other family, and I started thinking more and more about home. By this time, I had been away for more than a year.

I used to say to Lee, 'I want to move back to England,' but he would always say no. You don't have to spend very long in Majorca to realise that most people working out there stayed because they were running away from something in the UK; there would usually be a reason why they didn't want to go back. There were lots of long-term workers, familiar faces on the strip, who had been living there for years and years, and probably didn't know any different, who had lost touch with any reality that existed for them before Majorca.

Lee was from Worthing in West Sussex, and, although he wasn't running away from anything, he had been out in the Balearic Islands for a few years and was settled, with no desire to go back home. Life seems good when you have money and the sun shines every day. It was different for me – I couldn't imagine this life long term. I really loved my family and missed them so much. I told him I wanted him to move to Essex with me, but he used to say, 'No, babe, I'm staying here.'

I'd have my dad on the phone telling me I should come home if I wasn't happy, which just made it worse. The more I thought about home, the more miserable I became – Dad had been home in the UK for while, after his year job was finished, and I just couldn't hack it out there any more without family around me. I'd had such an amazing time and I'd grown up a lot, but I was still only 17 and a long way from home. It was only a few months until my 18th birthday, and I really wanted to go home. I begged and pleaded with Lee to come back with me, but he kept saying no.

Then, one day, I gave him an ultimatum. I remember we were lying in bed together one morning and I turned to him and said, 'I'm sorry, Lee, but I'm just not happy over here any more. I miss my dad and I miss my home – I've decided I'm going back.'

He replied, 'Well, if you've made up your mind, then I guess I'll have to come with you.'

I couldn't believe it – I was over the moon! After living this crazy life, I was finally going home. Lee sold his car, we quit our jobs, moved out of the apartment, said goodbye to all our friends and headed home.

We arrived back in the UK and rented a flat in Loughton, Essex. Lee got a job working in sales, which was what he had done before Majorca, and I started working for a courier firm in Blackfriars in central London. The money was good but the job was crap, and I hated it. I had a long commute into London every morning and then back to Essex again in the evening, and it was rubbish. After a few months, I quit and got a job working in a mobile-phone shop, near where we lived in Loughton. It sounds bizarre now, but it was the first mobile-phone shop in the town!

Now that I was back in Essex, I couldn't help thinking about Danny Chapman, who I'd had the brief romance with a year earlier. Things with Lee weren't great – he didn't really want to be in Essex and I think he resented me for making him move back.

That November, it was my 18th birthday and my dad gave me the best present I'd ever had – a gold Rolex watch that he'd bought for my mum 20 years earlier. I'd never seen it before – he had kept it hidden all that time because he'd been planning to give it to me on my 18th birthday. Originally, it had a leather strap on it but he had a gold bracelet made for it, especially for me. I loved it. When I saw it, I cried. He bought me ten driving lessons as well and I was chuffed to bits – all my friends had already learned to drive when they were 17 but I'd been in Majorca with my moped to get around, so I'd missed out. Now I was desperate to pass my test.

Lee treated me as well. He bought me a Louis Vuitton handbag, which was really pricey and my first ever proper designer bag – I took it everywhere with me.

The thing was, I still couldn't get Danny out of my head. Then, one day, about two months after I arrived back in the UK, fate brought us back together. A couple of Lee's friends from Sussex, who I'd met in Majorca a few times, had come up to London, shopping for the day, and I'd told them I'd take them to east London to meet my Nanny Daisy.

We were on the Roman Road, waiting to cross at a set of traffic lights, when a car slowed down to stop at the red light so we could cross. I don't know what made me look at the driver of the car, but I nearly fainted in shock when I realised it was bloody Danny Chapman! Of all the millions of people in London, he just happened to be at the lights at the exact same time as I was crossing the road.

I didn't know what to do, so I said to the people I was with, 'Oh my God, keep walking!' I told them it was my ex-boyfriend and not to turn around. Obviously, I wasn't going to tell them that I was still in love with him. As soon as I saw him again, I realised it was him I wanted and not Lee, so I decided to ring him – which in many ways was a very bad idea.

For a start, he'd told me that if he ever saw me in east London again he'd slap me, so I was shitting myself about what he'd say. Plus, I was living with Lee and here I was, pining for my ex. I didn't have his number any more so I rang my step-mum, Karen, and asked her to get my old address book from the top of the wardrobe. Straight away she asked why and whose number I was after. I had to admit that I was after Danny Chapman's.

'Oh, Chloe, I really don't think that's a good idea. Remember what happened last time. I think you should leave it,' was her reply.

But I told her I really needed to speak to him – after all, I couldn't get him out of my head – so she reluctantly gave me the number. My heart was pounding as the phone rang but he didn't answer, probably because he didn't recognise the number, and it went straight to voicemail.

For some reason, I left a stroppy message telling him I'd seen him down the Roman Road and said, 'I've been going to east London all my life, and I'm not going to let you dictate where I can go!'

As soon as I put the phone down, he immediately rang back and didn't mention my message or his threat that he would slap me if he ever saw me again. He just said, 'Where are you? Are you back in England?'

I told him I was working at the mobile shop in Loughton and he said he was coming straight over. I couldn't believe it!

I hadn't really thought it all through before I rang him but I certainly didn't imagine he would come straight over to see me, but he did. We walked down the High Street, chatting away and catching up, and he was even better looking than I remembered. He was so fit and I really fancied him. I had to admit to myself that I'd never really fancied Lee at all. Deep down, I knew being back in touch with Danny was a dangerous game because of where it might lead, but I couldn't help it.

Me and Danny started texting each other. Lee was totally getting on my nerves by this point and making me cringe. I hadn't really been attracted to him from day one and now all I could think about was Danny.

Just a few days after we'd met up again, I went on a night out and arranged to meet up with Danny. We ended up going back to his house and I slept with him. I'm a really loyal person and cheating is something I'm really against, but I just couldn't resist Danny. I felt I had let him go once, and I was being given a second chance so I grabbed it with both hands.

The next morning, I was dreading going home to face Lee. I had been out all night and not come home – I'd lied and told him that I'd stayed at my Nanny Daisy's because I was in east London. When I walked in the house, he had a face like thunder. He looked at me and said, 'Where the hell have you been?'

'I told you where I've been, I stayed at my Nanny Daisy's,' I said.

'No you didn't – I *know* you didn't!'

It turned out he hadn't believed me when I'd said I was staying there, so, before I got back in the morning, he had phoned my Nanny Daisy and asked if I'd stayed with her.

Obviously, she didn't have a clue what was going on and didn't think to lie, so she just said no, I hadn't been there. How stupid of me. Lee was going ballistic, wanting to know where I'd been and why I was lying to him. It was awful.

I didn't know what to do but I was sure by this point that it was Danny I wanted to be with, so I told him I'd been with Danny. He went mental, calling me every name under the sun – bitch, slag, the lot. Then he picked up the phone and said, 'Right, I'm gonna tell your dad!'

I was shitting myself. I knew he'd hit the roof. I told him that he could call him if he wanted but it wouldn't achieve anything; it was over between him and me, and it was Danny I wanted to be with.

Then Lee started screaming at me, 'I moved back here for you! How *could* you? I gave up everything to come back and now you're dumping me after just a few months. I've just bought you a really expensive handbag and everything.' He was so angry that he asked for the bag back, but there was no way I was giving it to him!

We had such an almighty row and then he told me that we had to go to Worthing to see his aunt. The visit had been planned for ages and he'd told his aunt and nieces that I was going with him. His nieces were a few years younger than me and I'd promised that I would give them some of my old clothes; they were really excited about me going down there. I told Lee after everything that had happened there was no way I was going with him, but he just shouted at me and really laid it on thick. 'They are expecting you to be there – you can't let them down. They want to see you; they'll be gutted if you don't turn up. How can you do that to them? After what you've just done to me, it's the least you can do!' he shouted at me.

I felt bad about what I'd done to Lee, so eventually I agreed to go. I'd just slept with my ex behind my boyfriend's back and the last thing I wanted was to go and see his family and make polite small talk. I had to sit in the car for two hours all the way down there while he yelled stuff at me like, 'You made me come home and now you've done this. How could you?' Then he'd go from being angry to being upset and crying, and then back to angry again. It was awful – I felt like the worst bitch ever.

When we arrived at his aunt's house, we tried to pretend everything was fine between us because he didn't want to tell them we were breaking up. It was horrendous. His nieces didn't notice but his aunt could clearly tell something was wrong and kept giving us funny looks. I totally did not want to be there at all and Lee knew that; he was just punishing me.

I then had the return journey to cope with, Lee shouting more insults at me and me just sitting there and taking it. He started being really nasty about Danny and saying that because I'd dumped him before it would never work out because he'd never really forgive me. I didn't care what he thought about Danny, I was totally smitten and I thought he was just being bitter. Anyway, I knew for certain I didn't want to be with Lee.

The next day, I was at work and he rang me, kicking off. He yelled, 'I'm going to come down your work and smash it up!' I was scared what he'd do next. In the end, he just came down, and we sat in the car and talked. I remember him turning to me and saying, 'Is it definitely over?' and I had to say, 'Yes, it is.' It was awful – we'd been together eleven months and he'd moved thousands of miles for me. I felt bad for Lee but he wasn't settled back in England anyway, and after we broke up he went straight back to Majorca.

Once my relationship with Lee ended, Danny and me got back together properly and for a while I was happy, but then he changed his mind again and dumped me. I don't think he'd ever really forgiven me for not coming back the previous year. Lee was right, after all.

Deep down, I knew it was my own fault because I'd dumped him the first time around and I just couldn't believe I'd ruined everything. I thought he was the love of my life – I didn't think I would ever meet anyone else again. I was absolutely heartbroken.

I sank into depression and couldn't be bothered at work so I lost my job and had to move back in with my dad in Collier Row. All I cared about was my heartache.

It wasn't long before I hit rock bottom and I spent most of the time crying over Danny – and I couldn't accept that it was really over. My heart was broken and I wasn't thinking straight. I even turned into a bit of a stalker. I used to ring him constantly, but he would just cut me off. I would ring his parents' house as well and they got really fed up with me – I just wanted to know what he was doing. Plus, I couldn't stand being back at my dad's house because I'd been living on my own for 18 months and being back at home was too weird.

One of my friends from school, Vicki, was having a bit of a hard time so her mum asked if I would like to go and live with them for a bit. They had a house in a village called Stapleford Abbotts in the Essex countryside, and I went to stay with them. Vicki was suffering from depression – although I didn't really know that at the time – and it started to rub off on me. I felt more and more depressed and I couldn't get Danny out of my head.

One night, I just wanted to switch off and I'd seen that Vicki's mum had some sleeping tablets so I decided to take one, thinking that I would fall into a deep sleep and forget about Danny for a while. Anyway, after a while, it didn't seem to be working so I took another one and then they both kicked in and I went a bit delirious. I thought they hadn't worked, even though they had, so I carried on taking more and more until, eventually, I passed out.

Next time I woke up, I was in a hospital bed. It was horrendous. Everyone thought I had tried to kill myself and, even though I tried to tell them I hadn't, they wouldn't listen. My poor dad was devastated; he came to see me in hospital and I'd never seen him so upset. He kept on saying I should have talked to him but I kept telling him I hadn't meant it. So there I was, after having the time of my life living in Majorca, being totally independent, now back in England with nowhere to live and no job, and everyone thinking I was suicidal.

CHAPTER FIVE

Settling Down

After the 'attempted suicide', I decided that I had to sort my life out and stop pining over Danny. Although I would never forget him, I knew that I needed to get on with my life – I was still only 18. I landed a job as a manager of a clothes shop in Bow, east London. My dad helped me out and I got a small flat in Buckhurst Hill in Essex.

The girls I worked with used to go clubbing in the West End and told me tales about all the celebs they would see. It sounded so much better than any of the places in Essex. One night, they asked if I wanted to go with them and I jumped at the chance. I got myself all glammed up and we went to Sugar Reef in Soho, which was the trendiest place to be back then. As usual, I wore something totally different to anyone else – it was a Burberry checked outfit years before people started wearing Burberry!

As the girls and me stood there chatting, a guy walked past, tapped me on the shoulder and said, 'You're beautiful.'

I shrugged him off but, as soon as he turned to walk away, my friend said, 'Do you know who that is?' It was Frank Lampard! I'd no idea – I was totally clueless, I didn't even understand what Premiership footballers meant back then. My friends then pointed out that Rio Ferdinand was over in the other corner.

Everyone told me Frank Lampard telling me I was beautiful was a big deal, and it was the first time that I realised perhaps all those people at school had been wrong and I wasn't ugly after all. It dawned on me that maybe I could use my looks to get what I wanted. As I went back to Essex at the end of the night, I was over the moon – it might have been just one comment but, still, a footballer had told me I was beautiful!

I had started to feel more confident about the way I looked but there was one thing that was bothering me. I was flat-chested and all the other girls seemed to have really big boobs. I'd always been conscious of my small boobs but then it started bothering me more and more.

Not long after that night, I went out with a friend called Katie, who was from east London, and we met up with her boyfriend and some of his friends. One of them was called Matthew and he was really nice. He was good-looking, with dark skin, blue eyes, and he had a really nice smile. Matthew was 24, so a few years older than me, and he was well dressed and seemed like a nice guy. My friend Katie was keen for us to get together so we could go on double dates. She could see he liked me and encouraged me to go for it!

He asked if he could take my number and, a few days later, he rang and asked if he could take me out. Matthew lived in Poplar in east London and he came to Buckhurst Hill to pick me up in his BMW. He lived with his mum and dad and he had a job working as a builder with his dad.

We went out for a drink. He was really nice but there wasn't a spark and, although he was good-looking, I just didn't fancy him. Because I'd had such a spark with Danny, I kept thinking that it wasn't good enough just to like someone. Matthew kept ringing me and I tried to put him off a few times but eventually I agreed to see him again. I told him I wasn't really interested. Looking back now, I was still hung up on Danny.

All my friends told me I was mad; they kept saying he was much nicer than Danny and that I was crazy not to be going out with him, when he clearly liked me. They kept going on at me about how lovely he was and how I hadn't given him a proper chance, so, eventually, I agreed to go out with him again. I decided I had to stop comparing him to Danny and to just relax and get to know him.

This time, we got on a lot better. We went to a local pub and had a few drinks, and he was really funny. I laughed a lot that night. Matthew's got a piss-taking sense of humour like me and we had a laugh. I think the first few times we went out he was nervous, and I was being standoffish – that was why I hadn't noticed how funny he was before. It wasn't perfect, I still felt there was something missing compared to how I'd felt about Danny, but he was nice and we got on, so we started seeing each other.

Eventually, I got sacked from the clothes shop because I just couldn't really be bothered and again the travelling from Essex to east London every day was doing my head in. I got a job working at the Queens pub in Buckhurst Hill near my flat, which was much more convenient. Still really into fashion, I spent all my money on clothes; I'd even buy stuff and then alter it so no one had the same things as me. Although the pub didn't pay much, I liked it because it was sociable – there was always someone to talk to.

A couple of months before I met Matthew, my cousins, Nikki and Carly, had asked me if I wanted to go on a girls' holiday with them to Ayia Napa in Cyprus. I'd never been on a proper girls' holiday before – when I was out in the Balearics I was working, so it wasn't the same – and I told them I'd love to, but I was only working in the pub and couldn't afford it. I told my dad they'd asked me to go with them and he said he would pay for it for me. I couldn't believe it! After the whole 'suicide' episode, I guess he thought I needed cheering up and could do with a holiday. Over the years, Dad has always been great like that. Whenever I've needed him, he's been there for me.

As soon as he told me he'd pay, I got straight on the phone to Nikki: 'My dad said he'll pay for me so I can come with you!'

We were screaming with excitement. Carly is a year older than me and Nikki is just a few months older – they are really close in age. For most of the year, Nikki and me are the same age but, when it's her birthday, I always take the Mick out of her for being old! We've always been really close because we are such similar ages and I couldn't wait to go away with them – we were going to have a right laugh.

These plans were made before I'd met Matthew but, now he was on the scene, he didn't want me to go. He was jealous and possessive, and begged me not to go. I was torn because I really, really wanted to go but I didn't want to upset him.

I rang Nikki and told her that Matthew didn't want me to go and she had a right go at me. I remember saying to her, 'Nikki, I've got a problem – I don't think I can come to Ayia Napa with you and Carly. Matthew's not happy about it.'

Well, she went off on one, saying, 'I can't believe you're dropping us for some bloke! You've known him two minutes and we've had this holiday planned for months, and now you're saying you're not coming. What a liberty!'

Now I love Nikki, but she is not someone you mess with and was quite scary, so I told her I would still go. And, anyway, she had a point – it's not right to drop your mates just because you've got a new fella.

It was the best holiday ever. We were young, free and single, and we were out every night. I have never laughed so much in all my life as I did that week – it was mental. We spent the days lounging by the pool, chatting and laughing, and then every night we'd get all dressed up and go round the bars and clubs. It was amazing – I loved it over there. The weather was boiling, the beaches were gorgeous and the bars and clubs were great.

I had such a good time and we all said we would definitely do it again – I didn't know then that this would be my last girls' holiday for seven years!

I missed Matthew and I had a niggling worry at the back of my mind that, because I'd come away when he was so against it, maybe he would go off with someone else. I rang him every day while we were away and, because I missed him, I decided that must have meant I liked him more than I had first thought.

When I got back from Ayia Napa, things with Matthew soon became serious, even though I still wasn't 100 per cent sure about him. It was weird – he was good-looking, funny, had a decent job, hung around with a cool crowd – there was no reason not to like him, but there was just something missing. When I look back now, it wasn't right from the start, but everyone else being so positive about him meant that I didn't acknowledge it.

I was a free spirit and I enjoyed working in the pub, flirting with all the customers. It really suited me, but Matthew hated it; he didn't like me chatting to other men and, as such, we had a volatile relationship. He had a real temper and used to shout and swear – he would kick off at the slightest thing and go mental. The first time, it really shocked me, he was swearing every other word – my dad never ever swore in front of me because he is old-fashioned like that – and I'd never heard swearing in anger like that before.

He would always apologise afterwards, saying how sorry he was, so I'd forgive him. After only a month of being together, he moved in with me and I became reliant on him. I couldn't drive – I'd had the ten lessons my dad bought me and I was absolutely rubbish so was nowhere near passing my test – and I had hardly any money. The flat we lived in was damp and cold, and neither of us really liked it there.

Then Matthew stopped working so we were really skint and were forced to move in with his mum and dad, Joan and Brian, in Poplar. I got on really well with them and we all became close, but living with your boyfriend's parents is never ideal. I should have been going out, enjoying myself but instead I was either at work or at home with my boyfriend's mum and dad!

Although I liked working in the pub, the money was rubbish and if we were ever going to move out of Matthew's mum and dad's, I needed a better wage. As a result, I got myself a job at House of Fraser in Victoria, selling make-up and perfume. I hated it. Again, I was faced with the long commute into London and I hated doing other people's make-up – I didn't like touching their faces.

I felt like I was trapped – as much as I liked Matthew's parents, it was hard all living together and we used to have almighty rows. We would literally be screaming at each other and he would shout insults at me. He was jealous of my relationship with Danny, and he used to say horrible things and call me flat-chested, which he knew really got to me.

We had an explosive relationship – I would scream and shout just as much as Matthew. I know it bothered his mum especially – it can't have been nice for her to have us yelling at each other all the time. Things weren't going great; I didn't want to be living there and I knew they didn't really want us there, but we didn't have any money to move out.

Then, when I was still only 19, the worst thing I could have imagined happened: I fell pregnant. It was awful. I'd been a bit rubbish at remembering to take my Pill and then I started feeling really ill and missed my period. I couldn't believe it; I was devastated. I went out in my lunch hour to buy a test because I needed to know. When I saw it was positive, I just sat in the toilets at work and cried.

I was lost; I didn't have a clue what to do. How on earth could I even think about having a baby? I definitely didn't want to keep it, but I didn't dare think of getting rid of it either – I just wished I wasn't pregnant. I didn't want to be pregnant; I wanted it all to go away. Deep down, I knew things weren't right between Matthew and me, and having a baby was a terrible idea. I was so young, with so much left to achieve and I still dreamed of becoming a model.

I had to tell Matthew, but I was dreading it. I told him that night after work; that I'd made up my mind and I was having a termination. He told his mum and dad, but I didn't tell anyone in my family. His mum and dad were really good about it; they respected the fact that it was our decision and they didn't try to influence us either way. As much as they would have loved a grandchild, they knew how young I was. Matthew became really distant and the rows got even worse. He started going out more and more – he basically abandoned me and I couldn't stand it, which meant we'd fight even more.

The day of the abortion came around quickly. Matthew took me to the place and just left me there. It was horrible, and I have tried to blank out all the details from my memory. I did my best not to think about it – I just wanted it to be over so I could try to forget it had ever happened.

When they said I was allowed to leave, I rang my Nanny

Linda and told her what had happened; she told me to go back there. She was such an amazing woman I could tell her literally anything, and I knew she would never judge me. I got a taxi over there and I've never been so relieved to see her in all my life.

The next day, I decided I needed some company because I didn't want to be on my own, thinking about what I'd done. So I went to meet my cousin Carly – I caught the train to Bethnal Green, where she lived. She wanted pie and mash, so we walked to Pellici's on the Bethnal Green Road. It was quite a long walk and, looking back, I wasn't up to it but I went anyway because I thought the fresh air would do me good. And I didn't want to admit to myself that I didn't feel right because I didn't want to think about what I'd done; I needed to feel normal and pretend everything was OK.

When we got into the pie and mash place, I started feeling really unwell. I stumbled into the toilet and realised I had blood pouring out of me – there were literally clots the size of strawberries – and I didn't know what to do. I could barely walk, I felt so weak and I remember calling out to Carly. I was saying, 'Carly, I really don't feel well,' and she thought I was exaggerating. She was saying, 'Don't be daft, Chloe, come out of the toilet!' I told her I couldn't and I think then she realised something was seriously wrong. She phoned for a cab and somehow managed to get me into it and took me straight to the Royal London Hospital in Whitechapel.

I was haemorrhaging and it was horrific. They put me straight on a drip and I was really scared. I blamed myself for having the abortion and just wanted the whole thing to go away. I couldn't get hold of Matthew so I rang his mum and dad and they came to see me. Matthew never came.

They kept me in hospital for a week; it was horrible in there. As if I hadn't been through enough with the abortion, I had to have a scrape because they thought maybe there was something left inside me that had caused me to haemorrhage. Matthew's mum and dad came and listened to me crying but Matthew still didn't come, and, for that whole week I was in hospital, I didn't hear from him. I was so upset; I really wanted him to be there. I couldn't ring any of my family because I didn't want them to know what had happened; I blamed myself constantly and I didn't want other people knowing. Some days, I only had the nurses for company – luckily, they were really kind to me.

Finally, on the day I was being discharged, Matthew turned up to pick me up and take me home. He said he was really sorry. I remember him saying, 'I know I've been a complete arsehole and I'm sorry. Please forgive me.' He promised me things would be different and he'd sort himself out. We went back to his mum and dad's for a while longer. He got himself a job then we eventually found a really lovely flat in Epping. For a while, things were good. We had money so we could go out for meals and do the stuff normal couples do. Although I wasn't head over heels for Matthew, he was my best friend and we spent all our time together. We were really close, even though we fought all the time. Looking back now, it was more like a brother and sister relationship.

I got a job working at Chanel in the West End and I started working quite long hours. I had to keep myself busy

– it was far easier to work all the time with less time to think about what I was doing. Sometimes I would get a niggling doubt at the back of my mind, where I thought, 'I don't want to be with him,' but I felt stuck in that life so I made the best of it. Although he promised to turn over a new leaf, Matthew was always going out and would often stay out all night and not come home. Despite it all, I just couldn't imagine not being with him, so leaving never really seemed like an option back then.

The following spring, we went on our first couple's holiday to Marbella and it was a complete disaster. It should have been a lovely romantic holiday but it was horrendous. On our first night there, we went for a night out in Puerto Banus and Matthew bumped into some guys he knew from back home. We ended up spending the night with them and the drinks were flowing – people just kept presenting me with more drinks. In the early hours of the morning, I was getting tired and wanted to go back to the hotel but Matthew wouldn't come. He was so busy trying to impress these so-called friends, so I went back on my own and went to bed.

The next morning, he dropped a bombshell: he had spent all our money for the whole week the previous night! It turned out that he had been buying all the drinks for the whole group – I just assumed that he'd been taking it in turns with the other guys. I'd worked hard for months, saving up enough spending money so we could have a nice time and he'd just blown it all in one evening.

I was absolutely livid. It just showed how immature he was – he was so busy showing off that he'd spent literally every penny we had. He ruined that holiday because he was trying to play the big man. We had massive rows and I hated him for that; we should have been having a lovely holiday but instead we had literally no money and could barely afford to eat for the rest of the week. We couldn't do anything. It was awful and we were miserable, so we just argued more and more as the week went on – made even worse by the fact we were in each other's pockets and neither of us could escape to work!

I kept thinking back to the girls' holiday I'd been on to Ayia Napa with Carly and Nikki. It had been such a laugh and I'd had such a fantastic time. The whole week I was in Marbs with Matthew, I was remembering those days in Cyprus and what a good laugh the girls and me had had – I wished I was with them.

After that holiday, I knew in my head that I had to dump him, so I did. At least I tried, but, every time I told him that I wanted to leave, he would talk me out of it and promise me the world, so I ended up staying. Sometimes he would even cry.

And then, just a few months later in June 2001, my whole world was tipped upside down.

CHAPTER SIX

Bad Times

'I've got some bad news – Auntie Tina has gone missing,' said my dad on the phone.

'What do you mean, missing?' I asked, but no one had any answers.

When I was growing up, Auntie Tina had been my surrogate mum and I just couldn't understand what was going on. Where was she? This was all a bit too close to home after what happened with my own mum, and I just couldn't bear the thought of losing someone so close to me again.

I started thinking back to all those years before, when I used to go and stay with Auntie Tina and Uncle Donald. I remembered helping her choose what stuff to buy and to decorate the nursery with when she was pregnant with Frankie.

All those hours I'd sat in the nursery, staring at the cot and waiting for the baby to come.

Then my thoughts flashed to Frankie being born when I was six – she was the prettiest baby with blonde hair and big blue eyes. Then, a few years later, Auntie Tina had Joey, when I was nine. He was another gorgeous baby with the same blonde hair and blue eyes. I loved my two cousins to bits – I was the boss and I used to mother them. I'd missed out on any siblings in my early years, but I'd grown up with my cousins and we were really close. We were always having sleepovers – our favourite film was *Drop Dead Fred* and we'd all sit together on the sofa and watch it, eating sweets. I would always be stealing their sweets, using the fact I was the eldest to be in charge – I liked to use power to my advantage!

When my brother came along when I was 12, followed by my half-sisters – Frances a year after that, and Demi another year later – there were six of us and we were a proper gang. We used to get together all the time. Tina was my dad's sister and they were also really close. Then, of course, there was Tina and my dad's mum, our Nanny Linda, and then Nanny Linda's mum, Nanny Daisy, who kept everything together. We were such a close family, a real force to be reckoned with – I couldn't bear the thought of anything changing.

Tina was the most beautiful, classy, amazing, kind woman I've ever known. She always looked nice; she had long, dark hair and she was so pretty. She always seemed so glamorous. She read *Vogue* and would show me the latest fashions in the magazines, even when I was too young to know what it all really meant. When I used to stay over at their house, me,

Frankie and Joey would all sneak in her bed, leaving poor Uncle Donald to find somewhere else to sleep. She was a good cook and her house felt cosy and welcoming.

The fact she had been willing to take me on when my mum left just shows what a lovely person she was. She was so young at the time, but I really think she would have done it as well – she would have given up her single life to be a mum to me and I will never, ever forget that. Yet here I was at 20 being told that my beloved aunt was missing. She just disappeared from their house in Chigwell in June 2001 and no one knew where she had gone or what had happened.

Frankie was 14 and Joey was just 10. I couldn't bear the thought that anything had happened to her. I just kept praying, 'Please, God, let her be OK.'

The waiting was terrible. Uncle Donald brought Joey and Frankie to my dad and Karen's house, and I remember Joey saying to his dad, 'Where's Mummy gone?' It was just awful. Uncle Donald was telling Joey that she would be back soon, even though no one had any idea whether she would be or not.

We were all just waiting and hoping for some good news. I took my Nanny Linda some food because she had been waiting by the phone but there was still no news. As soon as I arrived at her house, I knew something had happened as my dad's car was outside. I had only spoken to her 15 minutes earlier and she had said no one was there, which is why I was taking her food.

Tina had been found, but she was dead. My dad and Nan were both sitting in silence; it was like they were broken. I've never felt a chill of complete sadness run through my nan's cosy house as I did that afternoon. When I walked through the door, my dad told me and I dropped everything I was carrying; I was in complete shock. As I walked in further, I saw my nan hunched over in her kitchen chair, silently sobbing. I didn't know what to do. I'd never seen my dad cry before – he's a strong man and he had never shed a tear in front of me.

Within minutes, Uncle Donald arrived. Matthew had gone to my dad's house to pick up Frankie and Joey. They were all there with Karen and my little brother and sister, unaware of this heartbreaking news.

I remember clearly Frankie and Joey walking in. When Donald told them, they screamed and Joey just collapsed. It was the most heartbreaking thing I've ever witnessed. She was gone; my family was in despair.

All I cared about was being there with Frankie and Joey. I slept at my nan's in bed with Frankie for nearly a week. I used to lie there stroking her face, secretly checking for tears.

Auntie Tina had been like a mother to me and I'd wished she was my mum; she was an amazing mother to her own children and I knew their lives would never be the same again.

Although I was only 20, I felt that I needed to be there for them as much as I could, so, within just a few weeks, me and Matthew moved to a flat in Chigwell, just one street away from their house and round the corner from them. I decorated the spare room for Frankie so that she could come and stay whenever she wanted. She was a teenager, such an important time in her life. I needed to be there for her; I felt like she needed me.

I felt very strongly that I had to be there for Frankie and Joey to repay Tina for everything she'd done for me. It was as if this was my chance to show her just how much I appreciated the way she had always looked out for me.

Matthew was great throughout the whole thing – he loved Frankie and Joey, too – and he was great with the whole family. He became less aggressive and things were good between us; he realised that I needed to be there for my family and he never complained. He knew how upset I was and he did his best to avoid arguments.

As time went by, Matthew became part of the family. Things settled and it was so comfortable between us that I stopped thinking about the niggling doubts I had. Then he started dropping hints that he was going to propose. I kept telling him to shut up – not because I didn't want him to pop the question – but because I wanted it to be a total surprise. He has always been really crap at keeping secrets and he was ruining what should have been a special surprise.

My uncle Donald – Frankie and Joey's dad – has got connections with jewellers and has always been able to get really good deals, so Matthew had asked him to help find me a ring. Matthew kept winding me up, saying, 'I'm meeting up with Don today,' and then disappearing off. It was really annoying me because I had in my head that I wanted a big romantic proposal that came completely out of the blue – I didn't want him to keep going on about it.

Anyway, one night, we were at our flat and we'd had a row about something – I can't remember what. I was sitting in the bedroom, crying. Matthew just walked in, carrying the ring box, opened it and said, 'Will you marry me?'

It was not romantic and it wasn't how I'd imagined it. This wasn't the big sweep-me-off-my-feet moment that little girls dream about. I was gutted. Matthew knew I had wanted it to be really romantic, but the ring was perfect – Don had got a good deal – it was a gorgeous diamond and I loved it.

Despite the unromantic proposal and all my thoughts about Matthew not being right, I was very excited about being engaged. I thought I really didn't have any choice; I assumed this was it forever. I used to think about breaking up with him but it seemed like such a hard thing to do. I'd broken away from all my friends, I had no money and I couldn't drive; I had become dependent on him.

Also, I was still devastated about Tina, and Matthew was trying to be there for me. He really loved me and I really thought I loved him, so I put any doubts I had to the back of my mind and tried to focus on the good points. Because I'd been with Matthew since I was so young, I just thought that's what relationships were like. I felt that I'd made my bed so I had to make the best of it. I was the perfect little wife – I'd do all the cooking and cleaning and was really house-proud. Matthew would go out to work and do all the DIY and man jobs. Being a builder meant he could turn his hand to anything.

Our flat was above a parade of shops on the main road in Chigwell and it wasn't ideal, so we worked as hard as we could to save money so we could buy our own place. Around this time, I left Chanel and got a job working in an ironing shop in Chigwell, which was one of the worst jobs I've ever had. It was close to home so I no longer had the long commute into London every day, but I had to sit there all day ironing, with this great big industrial iron. I was covered in burns. It was hardly surprising that I didn't stick with it for long. I quit and got a job working in a clothes shop in Chigwell instead. I really liked my boss and she had a little boy called Louis, who I used to help look after.

I spent a year working six days a week and had no spare cash. I had so little money; I'd never go out and would spend night after night just sitting in the flat. I used to stay in all the time – looking back now, I realise I was growing old before my time. I was so tired from working that I couldn't be bothered to go out once I'd got home. Matthew would go out with his friends, but he never took me with him; I wouldn't be invited along. He did loads of stuff, went to V Festival, concerts, you name it, but it was always just him and his mates. So there I was, sitting at home on my own, while he was off having fun. I didn't have a car and, after a long day's work, I couldn't be bothered getting the bus anywhere to go out, and I was too skint to afford cabs.

Once we had enough money for a deposit, we bought a little starter home on an estate in Hainault, which wasn't far from Chigwell. It only had one bedroom and was tiny, but it was ours and it was quiet. A big change from our little flat and it felt really grown up.

I left my job in the clothes shop because it was becoming too much for me – I was working long hours and then looking after little Louis all the time, and it wasn't fair on me. I got a job working as a receptionist at a fashion company in Brewery Road in Islington – they did all sorts there, from designing to pattern cutting. Around then, I started getting more and more into fashion and I began making my own clothes.

Then I started buying odd bits of fabric and making them up into patchwork bags; they were really cool and I really enjoyed it. I decided that was what I wanted to do, so I looked into getting myself a stall on one of the markets. I ended up with a stall in Spitalfields market in east London. Spitalfields was full of people in a similar situation, selling things they'd made themselves – all sorts of cool things, clothes, jewellery. At weekends, it would get packed out with shoppers.

It was great having the opportunity to sell my own creations and the bags sold really well, but soon it became too much for me. I was working all week at the fashion house and then at the weekends I'd be working on the market stall. Working seven days was exhausting, and I knew I had to keep the regular money coming in, so reluctantly I gave up the stall.

Once, I was walking down Brewery Road after work in the dark on my own when something very random happened, which would come back to be important years later. There I was, walking along this dark road, when a car slowed down and pulled up alongside me. I was shitting myself; it could have been any kind of weirdo. I remember it was a BMW and a black guy got out and walked over to me. When he got closer, I realised it was Simon Webbe from the boy band Blue. I couldn't believe it!

At the time, Blue were really famous and I was in total shock. I remember he said to me, 'Are you a model?'

I said I wasn't, but I told him how I'd always wanted to be one. He explained that he ran a modelling agency in Manchester called Industry People and he gave me his card and told me to ring his manager, who ran the agency up there.

Well, I was totally speechless. I'd been dreaming of being a model for years, and here was a real-life pop star stopping me in the street and offering me the chance to make all my dreams come true!

I'd been getting really frustrated working at the fashion house surrounded by models and then here was someone offering me a chance – it felt like fate. I was so excited I rang the number on the card the next day and spoke to the lady who ran the agency. I explained what had happened and she said it all sounded great, but then she dropped a bombshell: I would have to move to Manchester, as that was where they were based.

When I put the phone down, I felt so deflated because I knew I couldn't do it. I was engaged to Matthew and we had a mortgage to pay. Then there was my family; I was too tied down, I had responsibilities. There was no way I could just drop everything and move up North, so I had to say no.

I couldn't believe I was turning down such a golden opportunity. It seemed that, over the years, opportunities had come up, but always at the wrong time and I had always missed out.

CHAPTER SEVEN

Madison

'Shit, this can't be happening!' was my first thought. And then, 'Shit, shit, shit!'

I was pregnant.

I couldn't believe it. I could not believe I had been so stupid. What on earth had I done? Why, oh why, had I been so stupid?

I'd left the fashion house and got myself a job working in the City as a receptionist. I was working for a property firm who rented out office space to different companies and my office was in St Paul's. It was a long commute so, when I started feeling really knackered and a bit sick in the mornings, I just put it down to the long days and the new job. Then, one lunchtime, I went outside for a cigarette; as I lit up and started to smoke, I couldn't stand the taste of it. That was when I knew. I remembered the symptoms from when I was pregnant before, and I just knew I'd been caught out again.

For the rest of the day, I was in a complete daze. I couldn't believe it; this couldn't be happening again. The whole way home, I had a knot of fear in my belly. I didn't want to take a test because I didn't want to confirm my fears and for it all to become real, but I knew I had to.

As soon as I got home, I just came straight out and said to Matthew, 'I think I'm pregnant.'

He rushed round to the chemist to buy a test. He was only gone for a few minutes and, with no point putting it off any longer, I went straight to do the test when he got home. Sick with dread, I sat there in the bathroom.

Even though I knew deep down that I was pregnant, when I saw it was positive, I still couldn't quite believe it. All I could think was that I just wanted it to not be happening. I was so angry with myself for putting myself in that situation, especially as I knew things weren't the way they should have been with Matthew. When I look back now, I always knew I didn't feel the way I should have about him, but I tried so hard over the years to ignore those niggling doubts. Discovering I was pregnant, again, with his baby meant that now the doubts were all I was thinking of: things just weren't right.

Matthew's temper and my reactions to it meant that we would fight like cat and dog, and I knew this wasn't the right environment to bring a child into. But I was totally torn and I really didn't know what to do. On the one hand, I just didn't want a baby with Matthew, but, on the other, I had already had one abortion and then I'd had those terrible complications. I was petrified of going through anything like that again.

I kept thinking this might be my only chance to have a baby. Imagine having a second abortion and then not being able to have kids – I couldn't take that risk. I'd always wanted a family, but I was still only 22 and I didn't feel ready for such a massive life change. Despite all my doubts, I gave up smoking on the day I did that test.

In contrast, Matthew was really excited. He thought it was great news. At 28, he was older than me and for him it seemed like the obvious next step. Most of his friends had settled down and a lot of them had kids already, so he assumed it was the natural progression for us. Despite being older, Matthew was still pretty immature and I could tell he was just thinking it would be a cute little baby.

I had seen the reality from my cousins and younger siblings but Matthew didn't know what was involved. He wasn't thinking about the responsibility and the hard work that having a baby, and then a son or daughter, entailed. I knew what it was like, I'd seen it first hand – the sleepless nights and the loss of freedom.

Even now, he doesn't really know what it's like to be responsible for a child because he has always got his mum and dad to help out. He basically lives the life of a single man and does what he wants, when he wants. He tells me he's proud of the way I have raised Mady and makes promises to help me out more, but unfortunately that doesn't pay the bills.

I also knew that other people would think it was great news – we had been together for nearly five years, we were engaged and we had our own place – it would seem like the next logical step. On the surface, it all looked great, but no one else knew how I really felt deep down. I had hardly even admitted it to myself; I just wasn't in love with Matthew.

Matthew was adamant that we'd keep the baby. He told his mum and dad, but the only person I told was my Nanny Linda. She told me I had to tell my dad. I didn't want to tell him, I just couldn't face it. Nan was harsh and told me I had to do it, that it wasn't fair on him, being the last to know. The following Sunday, when we were all round at my dad's house for his birthday, Nanny Linda kept looking at me as if to say, 'Go on, tell him,' but I just couldn't. I think she knew I was going to bottle it, so she just came out and said, 'Chloe's got something to tell you.' I couldn't believe she'd dropped me in it! I gave her a filthy look, but she just shrugged and said, 'Everyone else knows – it's not fair.'

That forced me to just come straight out with it and my dad looked pretty stunned. We went out for a walk after dinner, on our own, just the two of us. He asked me how I felt about it and I was desperate to tell him the truth, but I didn't – I wanted him to tell me not to have it. Everyone else had said it was my decision, but they all thought it was good news. I thought Dad would be different, I thought he'd disapprove; I thought he'd tell me to get rid of it, that I was too young. If I was being honest with myself, I was hoping he would, because then there would be someone else on my side and I could have an abortion.

He was quiet for ages and then just said, 'This isn't what I wanted for you, Chloe, you're still young and you've got your

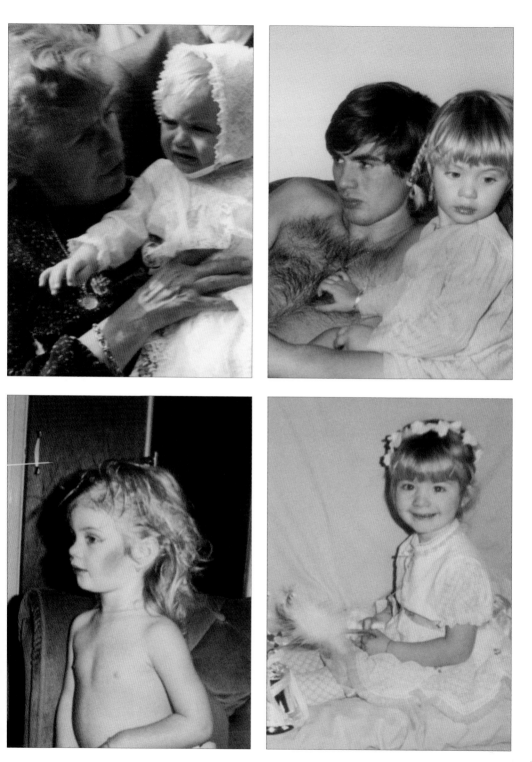

Above left: Me as a baby with Nanny Daisy, my dad's nan, on the day of my Christening.

Above right: Daddy's girl – this picture was taken when I was three years old.

Below left: Mini Essex girl in the making!

Below right: Already a poser.

Above left: My school picture at Brampton Manor in East Ham.

Above right and below: Growing up I was very close to my cousins, including Frankie and Joey.

At 15 I decided I wanted to
be a model. My dad let me
enter a competition in the
Romford Recorder.

I loved being in front of the camera.

Young single and ready to party!

Above: In 1998, after leaving school, I packed up my things and moved to Majorca, where I had the time of my life. From left: Nicky, Katie, Lucy, Rachael and me. Lee is just above me!

Below: In 2000, I headed to Ayia Napa for some fun. That's me on the left, before I had surgery, with Carly and Nicky.

I was 22 when I found out I was expecting Madison. Although Mady wasn't planned, I wouldn't change having her for the world.

Above left: One of the happiest days of my life: 23 April 2005.

Above right: Mady, Matthew (Mady's dad) and me.

Below left: Great-Nanny Daisy with baby Mady and me.

Below right: Nanny Linda, my dad's mum, with Mady and me. The relationship I have with Nanny Linda is what I imagine you would have with a mother.

Above: Brian and Joan, Matthew's parents, have been fantastic to me and Mady. It was Joan who suggested the name Madison to me. From left: Brian, Joan, Matthew and me.

Below: Celebrating Mady's first birthday.

Family has always been important to me.

Above: Me, my dad and my brother.

Below left: My sisters, Demi and Frankie, pictured with my brother and me in 2008.

Below right: Here I am with Auntie Tina, Nanny Linda and our friend Katie. Auntie Tina was such a glamorous lady.

whole life ahead of you.' He was really matter of fact about it and I was relieved he wasn't upset, but he didn't tell me what to do, he didn't tell me not to keep it. Then he looked at me and I saw a flicker of excitement in his eyes. He loves kids and, after all, this would be his first grandchild. I just couldn't tell him how I really felt about it. If anything, once the initial shock subsided, he actually seemed quite happy. I realised then that I couldn't tell him the truth, so, just as I'd been doing for ages, I kept quiet.

The next few weeks were torture; one half of me was saying, 'You don't want a baby' – I'd seen enough kids, my cousins Frankie and Joey, and my half brother and half-sisters Frances and Demi – to know that having a family was hard work. I mean, I loved babies and small children, but I also knew how tough it was. On the other hand, I kept thinking, 'I can't have another abortion.'

I carried on like that for a few weeks, arguing with myself, and then all of a sudden it was time for my three-month scan. And that was it, decision made. At that moment, it became real. I was lying on the bed and they put that cold jelly stuff on my tummy and then there it was, my baby, kicking on the screen. I could see arms and legs and everything, and all of a sudden I felt a rush of emotion so powerful it took my breath away.

It was love at first sight. In that split second, I knew I wanted that baby more than anything else in the world. My maternal instinct kicked in, and that was it. It didn't matter that Matthew wasn't the love of my life. Deep down, he was a decent man and this baby would make us stronger.

They told me I was due on 3 May 2005. They explained they would do tests to check everything was OK with the baby and would check for conditions like Down's Syndrome. As I waited for the results, I got myself into a right state. Things had changed and I really wanted this baby now but was torturing myself, thinking that, because initially I hadn't wanted it enough and had had bad thoughts, this would bring me bad luck. I thought Karma would come and get me, that something would be wrong, and that it would serve me right.

When the results all came back negative, I was over the moon. I became obsessed with doing everything by the book: I carried the scan pictures with me everywhere, showing them to anyone who would look. Then I bought loads of pregnancy books and became fixated on eating all the right foods and avoiding any that they tell you not to eat – I took it really seriously. I became so focused on the baby and followed the midwives' advice to the letter.

While I became this pregnancy-obsessed mum-to-be, Matthew changed, too. From the minute I told him I was pregnant, the rows stopped and it was as if he fell in love with me properly for the first time. He couldn't do enough for me, he was like the perfect partner: he wouldn't let me lift a finger, he would do everything for me and treated me like an invalid! For most of my pregnancy, he and I were happy – we felt real love for each other. We had a lovely time planning for the baby's arrival, decorating the nursery and buying all the things we needed.

I really wanted the baby and I really wanted us to be a proper family unit. By then, I really did love Matthew and I thought that would be enough. But, despite all that, I had an awful pregnancy: I constantly felt sick, and I was sick every day for months. Every day, I used to sit on that tube going to work in the City and I just felt so ill. And I was emotional – I would cry all the time, triggered by the smallest of things.

Life wasn't perfect: Matthew and me still had our fair share of rows, and towards the end of my pregnancy he even ended up in hospital after one argument got out of control.

That particular evening, we'd been at home watching telly, when I decided I was going to bed. Matthew would always stay up later than me, playing on his PlayStation, and it used to wind me up; he would get loads of food out of the fridge and have a picnic on the living-room floor, leaving all the mess for me to clear up the next day. Anyway, as I walked up the stairs to bed, I made a sly remark about him making a mess and he lost his temper. He said, 'Shut up, you slag,' and that was it – I flew into a rage. I am definitely no slag – I was heavily pregnant with his child and thought, 'How dare you speak to me like that!' I saw red. Before I knew what I was doing, I snatched a picture off the wall of the landing and threw it, like a Frisbee, at his head.

The frame smashed and cut his head, and he jumped up and started going mad, saying, 'You've killed me!' He was shouting, 'I'm going to die!' and then he ran out of the front door and into the street, screaming. There was loads of blood and he was really freaking out. I knew from the time I was hit by that glass in Majorca that your head bleeds loads so it looks worse than it is, but because he was going so mental it made me freak out, too.

I dialled 999 and an ambulance came and took him to hospital. They took his blood pressure and it had dropped, so they ended up keeping him in. It was nothing serious – he had just worked himself up into such a state, thinking he was going to die. For years after that, he thought he had a brain tumour. Looking back now, it's funny, but at the time I was panicking in case I had badly hurt him.

We had decided not to find out if we were having a boy or a girl, and, although everyone kept asking me what I was having, I was sure I'd made the right decision. It was sometimes frustrating not knowing and I had to buy everything in neutral colours, but I loved the suspense of waiting for the surprise when the baby finally came. Everyone seemed to be convinced I was having a boy; I just wanted the baby to be born healthy, but deep down I was secretly hoping it would be a girl.

Throughout my whole pregnancy, I had been dreading giving birth. I am really squeamish and I was dreading the pain as well. Although I had read all the pregnancy books, I'd tried not to read too much about the actual labour in case I freaked myself out. I'd finished work at seven months and I spent the next few weeks nesting and getting the house perfect. I wanted everything to be just right before the baby came along.

Then eleven days before my due date – just as I had put the finishing touches to everything – my waters broke. I remember being in a panic and phoning the hospital; they told me to go straight in, but I wasn't really in any pain at that point, so I had a bath and did my make-up. I might have been about to give birth, but I still had my priorities! There was no way I was going into labour without my make-up on.

After thinking I had been coping so well with this labour lark, all of a sudden, the pains started getting worse and worse, so Matthew drove me to the King George Hospital – the same place I had been born all those years before. My labour lasted for another nine hours. Matthew's mum and dad came, too, but my dad was on holiday. Now I know I'm a bit rubbish when it comes to pain but I was screaming for pain relief; I was begging for an epidural and eventually they gave me one but then they told me I had to keep still because otherwise it would fall out. Well, I was screaming at them, going, 'How on earth am I meant to keep still – I'm in labour!'

I was going mental, but eventually they told me it was nearly over, only they were going to have to cut me to get the baby out. By this point, I didn't care any more and just wanted it to be over. So I gave one last great big push and the next thing I had a baby. I was so worn out from giving birth that when she finally came out I just collapsed with exhaustion and didn't even ask if the baby was a girl or a boy.

Then Matthew started shouting, 'It's a GIRL!'

I could not believe it – a little girl after nine months of everyone predicting I was having a boy. I was so happy!

Then they told me to take more gas and air, and I couldn't work out what was going on. They explained I had to give birth to the placenta. I had no idea what they were on about, but I just did as I was told and out came the most disgusting thing I've ever seen.

Because they had cut me, I had lost a lot of blood and I was lying there, totally exhausted, when they brought my little girl over to me. They had cleaned her up and she was wearing the little outfit I had planned for her. Then they asked me if I wanted to hold her but, as I went to lift my arms, I just couldn't – I had no strength left.

They handed her to Matthew and he tilted her face towards me. I'll never forget seeing her face for the first time. She was perfect! But then the midwives started panicking because they couldn't control the bleeding so they called for a doctor to come and stitch me up. We waited for ages, with Matthew going backwards and forwards to our family, who were getting anxious, waiting for news outside. Matthew's mum, dad and his auntie Teresa and my Nanny Linda were all there – they had been there the whole nine hours!

Once the doctor had put endless stitches in me down below, and I'd finally stopped bleeding, they were ready to wheel us out – me first and then my little girl, wrapped up inside the cot behind me. I remember seeing everyone's faces as we were wheeled past them; they were all so excited.

At first, they wheeled us on to a ward full of other mums and newborn babies, but I wasn't happy with that. I demanded my own room – no way was I sleeping on a ward with my precious baby! What if she caught something?

They found me my own little room on the ground floor. It had double doors opening on to a garden. Everyone flooded in and I was assured by my nan that my dad – who was away on holiday – had changed his flights and was on his way back.

As everyone was leaving, Dad, Karen, my brother and my sisters came running in. My dad explained that the nurses had told them they couldn't come in because visiting hours were over, but he had persuaded them to let them see me for just twenty minutes.

When they left, that was it: I was all on my own. I remember the first time I picked her up, she was so tiny; I still had no feeling in my legs from the epidural. I couldn't even get myself up to go to the toilet, so I had to use a commode – I definitely didn't get much sleep that night.

So that was it, the day my life changed forever. It was 23 April 2005 when my baby girl was born. She is absolutely the best thing that has ever happened to me and I love her more than anything else in my life.

The following day, my Nanny Linda came back and brought me an entire roast dinner in hospital because she just loves feeding people and I think she was worried I would fade away. Then all the rest of the family turned up – my dad, Karen and the kids, and Frankie and Joey, as well as most of Matthew's family. My room was packed.

They wouldn't let me leave until the next day, and Matthew came with the baby car seat we had bought and we took her home. I couldn't wait to get out of there and get back to my little house, where everything was waiting ready for my baby.

Because I didn't know what sex the baby was, I had only bought neutral baby clothes in whites and yellows, but now I had a little girl I was desperate to dress her in pink and asked people to buy her some things. I still hadn't decided on a name, either. I couldn't decide between Daisy (after my great-nan) and Madison – a name that Joan, Matthew's mum, had come up with. I was worried about calling her

Daisy, as I knew my nan was in her nineties and wouldn't live much longer; I didn't think it was fair to call her after someone who would pass away, so I chose Madison, but usually I call her Mady.

As soon as we got home, the visitors started coming again. They all wanted to have a cuddle with Mady, but I was too scared to let anyone touch her. I was paranoid about germs and I didn't want people going near her; I guess it was my hormones being all over the place, but I didn't want to let her go. I became obsessed with germs – I would have anti-bacterial wipes everywhere, and I wouldn't let anyone near her unless they had used them. We were inundated with cards and presents, and it wasn't long before Mady had plenty of pink stuff to wear.

The first few weeks were a blur and it seemed there was always someone in our house – and it wasn't until Matthew and me were left on our own that the cracks began to show again. Where he had been so helpful and kind during my pregnancy, he totally changed once Mady was born. I suppose maybe he felt pushed out because I was so devoted to her. He didn't help me at all, and he began getting aggressive again and then the rows started to escalate.

Looking back now, I think I was suffering from post-natal depression but at the time I didn't realise anything was the matter. Babies are hard work, and I was doing it all on my own, and me and Matthew started arguing. Most of our arguments were in the night, over him not taking his turn to feed Mady then. I was exhausted and needed sleep, but he wouldn't help. He'd got a job doing loft conversions and, because he was working during the day, he refused to help out in the night.

Plus, he was really messy and I couldn't handle it because I was obsessed with cleanliness – it was like having another child to clean up after. I got really run down, I wasn't eating properly and I became fanatical about everything being perfect.

Although Matthew's mum and dad offered to look after Mady to give me a break, I wouldn't leave her – I didn't want anyone else looking after her because they didn't love her as much as I did. I thought no one else could look after her like I could; I was the only one who cared that much about her and so I was the only one who should have her.

The first time I left her, she was about three months old and it was my cousin's birthday. Matthew's mum Joan offered to babysit at my house, but I was anxious about leaving her, even though it was only for a couple of hours. I cried when I left the house.

We were still living in a one-bedroom place and it was too cramped with me, Matthew and Mady, so we sold our starter home. We'd been lucky with the rising house prices so we made quite a lot of profit on it. We bought a new car, put our savings in the bank and moved into a rented house that had three bedrooms. Unfortunately, it didn't make me any happier.

Every night I would lie in bed and think about leaving Matthew. I wanted out – I didn't want to have sex with him, and I didn't want to be with him. From the outside, my life looked perfect – I had a three-bedroom house, money in the bank, a nice car, nice clothes, a lovely baby and a good-looking fiancé – but inside I was miserable with him. Time passed and I still did nothing about it; we were just coasting along together, and then all of a sudden a whole year had gone by and it was Mady's first birthday.

I organised a massive party for her and went totally overboard. I made her a fairy castle cake and did party bags, all the works. I threw myself into organising it so I didn't have to think about everything else that was going on. All my family came and it was a lovely day. Mady looked like a little princess and I'm sure to everyone else it all looked perfect, but, in reality, it was far from it.

With Mady getting a bit bigger, I decided I needed to get some independence so I started having driving lessons again, but I was still hopeless. Then someone suggested maybe I should try learning in an automatic because they are easier to drive and I couldn't believe it. My first thought was: 'Why has no one told me about automatics before?' All of a sudden, it clicked, and I passed my test so I could finally have some independence.

I was also really unhappy with my body after having Mady – even though I'd lost weight, my stomach still stuck out – so I joined the gym in a bid to tone up. Mady was getting bigger now, so I would leave her in the crèche. I started noticing other guys in the gym and thinking about how fit they were, and then that would make me think even more about leaving Matthew. I would never in a million years have done anything but just the fact that I was window-shopping alerted me to the fact that something was definitely wrong, and I needed to do something about it.

Things went from bad to worse and we continued to grow

apart. We would have huge rows, with screaming and shouting, and I knew it was a bad environment to bring Mady up in. I didn't want her to grow up with all the rowing; I wanted to be a good mum and that meant doing what was best for her. I kept thinking, 'This isn't right,' but I just didn't have the guts to do anything about it. I kept thinking I'd leave him, but we'd been together seven years and I didn't know any different.

We had always had a volatile relationship and I knew that, as long as we were together, there would be rows. I didn't want that for my little girl.

Then, one night, we had an almighty row and I came out and said, 'I don't love you and I don't want to be with you.' I couldn't believe I'd actually come out and said it, but I couldn't hack it any more – I just wanted to be on my own.

I told him I was leaving and he begged me not to, but that was it: I'd done it. Once I'd said it out loud, there was no going back.

The next day, I went house hunting and found the perfect place for Mady and me. It was a two-bedroom cottage in Woodford – an old place with a lovely fireplace, and it was down a quiet street so it was nice and peaceful. As soon as I saw it, I knew it was the perfect place for my little girl and me, so I went straight to the bank to get the money for the deposit. We had put the profit from the house sale into a savings account so I was just going to use that, but as I checked the balance I had a massive shock: half of the money was gone.

In a massive rage, I rang Matthew and he confessed he had spent it. It turned out he hadn't been working for months but he hadn't told me. He had gone off every day pretending he was going to work and then drawing the money out of our savings, pretending he'd earned it.

I was absolutely livid – that was our money, and he had lied to me and wasted half of it. I told him I was having the rest because it was rightfully mine. As far as I was concerned, he had spent his half already. I told him it was definitely over, but he cried and begged me to change my mind. I felt bad that I was breaking his heart, but I had to do it – I knew I didn't want to be with him.

It was heartbreaking – I didn't want to take his baby away, but I had to. If we'd stayed together, I would have ended up hating him before long.

Once I knew it was definitely over, I went to see my dad, so I could explain it all to him. I wanted to do it face to face, and I knew he would be worried about me being a single mum. To be honest, I think he saw it coming because he could tell I wasn't happy, and, although he was scared for me, he was very supportive.

When I got the keys to my new house, I spent a month getting it all perfect for Mady and me. I had it decorated to my taste and waited until it was done before we moved in. That last month, I was so excited – I'd lie in bed every night and imagine how life would be. Back then, I was going to the gym every day. Mady went into the crèche for two hours, and I'd spend one hour training and another getting ready and reading my book. I used to read every day; I loved getting lost in fairytale fiction – it was an escape from my life.

Once my house was done, I took Mady, all the furniture and even the car. I left the house and didn't look back. At first, when I moved in, I was so content; this was what I wanted. Yes, I felt guilty about Matthew but that was the only downside. Everything was perfect and I felt so excited about what the future would hold, as if I'd been given a second chance. My body was better than before the pregnancy, I had everything in place; now I was finally ready to live my life!

Matthew, meanwhile, went out and got himself another job and asked me to give him a second chance. He came round to my new place and asked if he could stay, so I let him sleep on the sofa for a couple of weeks. Deep down, I knew it was over, though. I had no regrets, apart from the fact that I had hurt him. Finally, he accepted it and went back to live with his parents for a bit while he sorted himself out.

We arranged it so that I had Mady during the week and then, on a Friday, he could come and collect her, and take her to his mum and dad's in the car. We shared custody of our daughter, as well as the car – whoever had Mady also had the car because I didn't want her being ferried about on the bus.

I told him that if he wanted to see Mady he could come over any time – he was always welcome to see her whenever he wanted – there was no way I wanted any differences we may have had to stop him from seeing her.

After the split, Matthew went off the rails a bit and started going out even more than he had done before, and then he'd go missing for days. I think he was bitter and angry about everything, and, although I wasn't impressed at the time, I couldn't really blame him. Having been part of a couple for so long, I guess he just wanted to go out and have some fun, but he was also meant to be a responsible father to Mady and I needed him to be grown up.

I made it clear to him that he couldn't say he was having Mady and then let me down. At weekends, I made sure he took her to his mum and dad's so they could help look after her.

Joan and Brian were upset when we split up because I was part of their family – after all, we had been together a long time. I mean, I had lived with them soon after we first got together and they had been there for me when I had the abortion all those years earlier. They were also unhappy because of Matthew's reaction to the break-up. He was their son and he was really going off the rails, so, although they didn't blame me for it, they were disappointed it hadn't worked out between us.

Now they are fine and I have a great relationship with them both – we are still really close. I know I could phone them at any time of day or night if I needed anything and they would always help me out. Joan especially has been so good to Mady and me over the years and I really do see her as being like a mum to me. We have the kind of relationship I imagine a mum and daughter have, and I hope she feels the same way.

Mady is their life – she is their only grandchild and they still have her every weekend. She has always had that routine – she's with me during the week and then on a Friday afternoon she goes to her grandparents in Hainault for the weekend. They spoil her rotten and she loves going there. She is safe, loved and happy, and that's all that matters.

Breaking up with Matthew was hard, but it was definitely

the right thing to do. We've moved on and get on well as friends now. He has helped me out over the years and he's Mady's dad – she loves him, and that's what matters. However, he has never really had to take full responsibility for her – that has always been on my shoulders. He knows his mum and dad will have her at weekends so he can come and go as he pleases, being Daddy for the good times. I wouldn't swap what I have for the world but being a single mum is hard.

A few months after we split, I heard Matthew had been seeing other girls and then I knew that it was final; it was definitely over. Although I was the one who left him, and I knew I didn't love him the way I should, it was still hard to hear that he was seeing other people. He was all I'd known for so long; we had been together for seven years and we had a baby together.

Once I realised Matthew had moved on and was dating other people, I realised I had to get myself out there and get a social life. After all, I was still only 25, not 45! I'd been living the life of someone much older and had barely been out in years, which I knew was just ridiculous. I'd always been really outgoing and sociable and yet I'd turned into a boring granny who sat indoors all the time, which really wasn't me.

I had spent too long being responsible and sensible, and it was time to go out and start having fun – I needed to catch up on all those missed years when I'd been playing wifey to Matthew. But, instead of just going out down the local pub, I decided to do something a bit more adventurous: I booked myself a girlie holiday to Marbella!

CHAPTER EIGHT

Single Lady

I flew out to Marbella in May 2007 with a group of five other girls, including my friend Katie who had set Matthew and me up all those years earlier, and we hired a great big apartment in Puerto Banus. It was only a long weekend, and it might sound a bit dramatic, but I seriously feel like those few days away in Spain opened my eyes to a new life.

When my friends first asked me if I wanted to go, I was really excited and jumped at the chance. I still had money saved in the bank from the sale of the house, and after everything that had been going on in the past few months I thought I deserved a nice break and a chance to let my hair down. I hadn't had a girls' holiday since I'd been to Ayia Napa seven years earlier!

But then the reality of leaving Mady hit me – she was two years old and I had never left her for that long before. I asked Joan and Brian if they would have her for four days and they happily obliged. So, in the lead-up to going, I went and treated myself to some new clothes – I bought dresses and shoes and, although I was dreading leaving Mady, I was really excited. I was 25, newly single and ready to live my life. I hadn't been happy for a long time, and I really wanted to go away and have fun.

The night before the trip, I felt sick at the thought of leaving Mady. I put her in my bed and watched her sleep and considered not going. I was crying the next morning as I said goodbye to her, and then I cried all the way to my friend's house, from where we were getting the taxi to the airport together. All of the other girls had children as well, so they knew how I was feeling. They told me I shouldn't feel guilty – it was only a long weekend, after all – and I deserved to have some fun. Having a break would do me good.

So I tried to think positive, and once we arrived in Puerto Banus I started to get excited. It was the May Bank Holiday weekend, which is a real party weekend over there and it's really busy. The day after we arrived, it was the famous Champagne Spray Party at the Ocean Club, which is a massive social event over there. Tickets are quite expensive and, basically, you can buy a ticket or pay for a large white leather outdoor bed around the pool. With the bed, you get ten bottles of champagne, which you drink throughout the day and whatever is left you spray at each other at the end. It was unlike anything I had ever seen or experienced before. It was wall-to-wall glamour.

It's a playground for the rich and famous. All the guys looked like male models and the girls are like glamour models – massive hair, huge eyelashes, fake tan and, of course, they all wear heels by the pool.

And there I was, feeling totally inadequate. I just wanted to crawl under my sun bed and hide for the rest of the day. I had always been slim, but I hadn't lost all my baby weight, and I still had a flabby tummy and these tiny boobs; it was awful. I was standing there in my wedges with hardly any make-up on, with my flat chest and post-baby belly. Let's just say my kaftan stayed on all day.

I decided there and then that I would never feel like that again; I was going to go home and have a boob job. I vowed that I would come back again the following year a changed person: I would be just as glam as the rest of the girls. There was no way I ever wanted to feel so inferior again. So, I made a pact with myself that I would give myself a Marbella makeover. I'd get new boobs and smash the gym, and I vowed I'd be back the following year with enough confidence to take my kaftan off.

Back home, I'd been glued to a reality show that had been on telly the summer I'd had Mady: *Celebrity Love Island*. I would be sitting feeding the baby, looking at all the celebs living it up on a desert island. I never missed an episode and found myself having a secret crush on Calum Best, one of the contestants. As I was sipping champagne by the pool with my friends, I couldn't believe my eyes as Calum appeared behind me.

He looked really cool in a pair of long shorts and a baggy

vest. As he walked through the party, I watched girl after girl greet him with air kisses. Even the guys were high-fiving as he passed. I remember imagining in my head what it would be like to know him and be one of those girls.

During the last seven years when I'd been with Matthew, I had barely even been out to local bars. When I was watching the show the year before, I'd never imagined that I'd be single, in Marbella and with the celebrities I'd just watched on the telly.

I needed the toilet desperately after drinking champagne all day, but I'd been holding it for as long as possible because going to the toilet meant walking across to the other side of the pool in front of everyone. I felt so self-conscious; I would have preferred to wet myself there and then. To my horror, I noticed Calum was standing right near the entrance to the ladies' loos. My legs went to jelly, which made it even harder to walk as I was already bursting for the toilet, trying to avoid eye contact with anyone and to balance in my ridiculous sky-high wedges. I looked around for a way to avoid Calum but realised there wasn't one so I carried on walking, thinking, 'Oh my God, oh my God!' as I went.

As I passed, he called out 'excuse me' in the accent I recognised from the show and I froze for a second. I was too nervous to speak, so I flashed him a big smile and carried on walking. I made it into the toilets and must have spent at least five minutes in there. I remember looking in the mirror surrounded by glamorous girls, fussing with their appearance around me. After lifting my sunglasses to check my reflection, I could have kicked myself for going *au naturel* that day. The best I could do was put some lip-gloss on and smooth my hair down before I went back out to face the music; I knew Calum would stop me again.

When I came out of the toilet, I noticed he was still standing in the same place and there was no way to avoid him. As soon as he spotted me, he called out and asked, 'What's your name?'

I was in shock! I couldn't believe it. He had two friends with him, which added to my nerves, and I just wanted the swimming pool to swallow me up. 'Chloe,' I nervously said.

He then said, 'Take your sunglasses off, I want to see your face.'

Even though I could hardly speak, I laughed and said, 'No, I'm not going to take them off – I've been drinking all day!' He was persistent and kept asking me to take them off, but I didn't.

After a while, he laughed and said, 'I might see you later.'

As I walked off, my legs were even more like jelly; I literally ran back to where my friends were. In the back of my mind, I kept thinking, 'Please don't let him notice the cellulite on the back of my legs!' But my friends were excited for me when I told them.

That weekend away was the start of my new life. Suddenly, I was going to the same parties and nightclubs as celebs. I had my first taste of it and I didn't want the weekend to end. It also made me realise I had made the right decision in ending things with Matthew. There had never been a spark between us; I just couldn't admit it to myself before. I came back from Marbella full of excitement about changing my life; I knew I had to finish with Matthew once and for all. I also knew I needed to sort my look out, and I was determined to lose weight and glam up – I never wanted to feel frumpy and flabby ever again. My plan was simple: be skinny, tone up and have a boob job.

Mady had started going to nursery in the mornings, so I had a bit of time to myself and began going back to the gym again. I would go as often as I could, and I would spend as long as possible working out. I was adamant I wanted to be a size 6 and tone up my whole body.

As I started to notice the effects of the gym, I didn't want to ruin it by eating as much as I did before. I would eat nothing for breakfast, and then I would go to the gym and work out for as long as I could – I would literally be on the cross trainer until I couldn't breathe.

People started commenting that I had lost weight and it made me even more focused. Every time someone told me I looked thinner, I was determined to lose even more weight and look even skinner. I also started getting back into fashion and buying expensive clothes – I still had savings in the bank, and I was determined to look good. At this point, I changed my image by wearing tighter clothes to show off my new gym body. I wanted to be taken more seriously, but with a bleached-blonde bob it was hard, so I decided I wanted to become a bit more rock-chick instead of being mumsy, and to stand out from the crowd.

After being away from the party scene for such a long time, I wanted to find out where all the coolest places to hang out in London were. I asked my old school friend Helen, who was working in Mayfair, where was best to go and she told me it was Movida. Helen was the first friend I made when I moved schools at the age of 13, and we have been best friends ever since. She said it was the latest place to be and it was always in the celeb gossip magazines. The problem was, you had to be a member or be on the guest list. I didn't know anyone and had no idea how on earth I could get in, but I'd set my mind on it and I was determined I would get in there. During the week, I was a doting mum to Mady but the weekends were my time and I couldn't wait to go out!

I explained my dilemma to one of the girls at the gym but she laughed and told me that, because of the way I looked, I would have no trouble getting in. She told me to just march up to the door and guaranteed they would let me in. So, I rang Helen and explained what the woman at the gym had told me and we decided to try our luck that Saturday night. I spent ages deciding what to wear and eventually chose a pair of black dancer leggings, a tight top and a black leather jacket. I accessorised with hundreds of bracelets to get the overall look I wanted. I'm surprised I could lift my arms! Back then, no one was wearing leggings like that – I bought them on the internet because you couldn't buy them anywhere else.

I had spent ages doing my fake tan and my make-up and false eyelashes, and finally I was ready to go. My outfit was topped off with a pair of skyscraper heels, and I had this huge black handbag that had everything in it but the kitchen sink. We used to call it 'the bomb' because it had a drawstring at the top and, when I laid it out, the contents would explode everywhere. I would take everything with me – all the usual stuff, like lip-gloss, a hairbrush and perfume, as well as anything extra I might need, like eyelash glue and even fake tan and a mitt in case my tan streaked and I needed to do a touch-up job. Fake tan is like a religion for Essex girls – you can never be seen without it but you need to make sure it's perfect at all times!

Buzzing with excitement, Helen and me drove into London and decided we would just try our luck at getting in. We had no idea if it would work or not, but I talked her into giving it a go. We turned up about 10ish, which was totally un-cool in itself as clubs like that never get going until late, but we were clueless back then and had no idea.

As we strutted up to the door, these two guys were outside and told us they were members and asked if we wanted to jump the queue. I was delighted – we'd done it! We were in! We went downstairs into the club and it was really empty but we were just happy to be there. The club was really plush and everything about it looked expensive. Out of nowhere, the manager came over and introduced himself, then asked if we wanted to go into the VIP area. I couldn't believe our luck! There were bottles of champagne in ice buckets on the tables and he told us to just help ourselves.

It worked out even better than I had hoped. The manager was a really nice guy and he gave me his number and told me any time I wanted to go down there just to give him a ring. It was my first taste of the London scene and there was no way I was going to stop there – I was excited! I had made friends with the manager of the hottest club in town and he'd told me I could go there whenever I liked.

The following Saturday, me and Helen and another girl,

Vicki, and her friend all went back there together. We had told them how great it had been the week before and that the manager had told us he could get us in any time, so they jumped at the chance to join us.

I had bought myself a dress from All Saints especially. It was backless so I couldn't wear a bra with it, but because I had literally no boobs – I was a B-cup at most – I couldn't go without a bra because then I would have had no boobs at all! I wasn't eating much and I was really skinny, which made my boobs shrink even more, so I made myself a bra and it was literally two stuck-on cups with a load of air behind them to try to make me look like I wasn't quite so flat-chested. We arrived a bit later than the previous week and the club was almost full, with a massive queue outside but the manager beckoned us straight in.

It turned out to be a special event for London Fashion Week and it was absolutely heaving. We were ushered straight into the VIP area, which was packed out all ready. And there were plenty of celebs in there, too. I saw Arsenal footballer Freddie Ljungberg, Jade Goody's ex-boyfriend Jeff Brazier, as well as her then boyfriend Jack Tweed.

I was standing there with my glass of champagne, loving every minute of it, when all of a sudden a drunk Calum Best marched up to me, said hello and went straight in for a kiss! Before I knew it, I was kissing him back. It was only a month after I'd met him in Marbella and I couldn't believe I had bumped into him again. I couldn't believe my luck and was over the moon!

Calum had arrived when it was nearly the end of the night

and, after our kiss, he asked me to go back with him, but I knew he had a real reputation as a womaniser so I said no. He asked me for my number so I gave it to him – I saw him save it as 'Champagne Chloe'. He probably only did that because he had several other Chloes in his phone! We had a final snog and then he hugged me, and I remember thinking in my head, 'Please don't burst the air in my bra!' As I left the club, I felt on top of the world.

My friends and me jumped in a cab to take us back to Essex and within a few minutes my phone rang: it was Calum. 'Come back to my place in Chelsea,' he said.

'No,' I told him. 'I'm in a cab on the way back to Essex.'

'Tell the cab to turn round.'

'No!' I giggled. Although flattered to have heard from him so quickly, I am not that kind of girl but I went home really happy. I lay in my bed running through the night in my mind, and I fell asleep with a huge smile on my face.

Over the next few days, Calum was texting me constantly and he invited me to a cage fight with him. I was so excited because it was a proper date, not just snogging in a club, and I couldn't wait. It seemed amazing that I had fancied Calum since watching him on *Love Island*, but now I was actually going on a date with him! I treated myself to the perfect dress for a first date; it was black and tight with brooches all over it and went down passed my knees.

The cage fight was on a week night and, obviously, I had Mady but I was desperate to go. So, I asked my Nanny Linda to babysit. I told her it was so I could go on a date with Calum Best and it's fair to say she was none too impressed, because, although she didn't know anything about Calum, she remembered his dad George's reputation for being a womaniser. I remember her exact words of warning were: 'Just be careful, love – his dad was a right player and, if he's anything like him, you'll end up getting hurt.' She only had my best interests at heart, but I was on cloud nine so I didn't listen.

After settling Mady at my nan's, I went home to prepare for our first date. Once I was finally ready, I texted Calum to find out the plans for the evening. I got a text saying he'd been away doing a PA the previous evening and he'd been up all night, so he'd only just woken up. I was fuming and didn't even respond, despite him texting me a few times after the original text. There I was, all glammed up with nowhere to go – I was so disappointed. I went back to get Mady and, of course, my Nanny Linda smugly said, 'I told you so,' which didn't help.

Calum was really apologetic and the following weekend he asked me to go into London once more to meet him, so I decided to give him one more chance. We went to Movida again and he was with his manager, Dave Read. Years earlier, Dave had launched Jordan's glamour-modelling career, so I was excited to meet him.

But the night didn't go as I'd hoped. At the beginning of the evening, Calum had been all over me, but then he disappeared and I didn't see him again. It wasn't how I'd imagined it would be and I was annoyed. Adamant I wasn't going to get upset over him again though, I decided to just leave. I got a taxi back to Essex with my friends who had come with me, feeling disappointed all over again but determined not to cry.

I went to bed and tried to forget all about it, but the next thing I knew I was woken up by my phone ringing: it was Calum. It was 5.30am and he wanted to know where I was. He said he had come back to look for me, but I'd gone. I told him I had gone home and that I was in bed. He begged me to go to his flat in Chelsea; I said no because I was in bed, but he wouldn't take no for an answer. Then I told him I didn't know the way to Chelsea – I could only just about find my way to the West End – and I didn't have a Sat Nav so I'd never find it.

He was so persistent that eventually I gave in; he gave me his address and I said I was on my way. I got up, put my outfit from the night before back on, made sure I looked OK, then got in my car at 6am and drove into London. I got myself as far as the Embankment and then, when I saw a black cab, I pulled over and asked the driver if he would drive to Calum's Chelsea Harbour apartment with me following and I would pay him the fare when we got there. I didn't tell Calum I had to get a cab to direct me to his house, I just made out I had driven there by myself.

When I arrived, Calum was really pleased to see me. We sat on the sofa and he started kissing me straight away. It was obvious he must have been drinking all night but he didn't seem that wasted and he was really nice. He was asking all about me and I told him about Mady, and he said he loved kids – he even said he would paint his spare bedroom pink for her to sleep in. Looking back now, it's easy to see he was just feeding me lines, but I was naive and I believed every word of it. After ages of chatting and kissing, we moved into the bedroom as we were tired. Calum kept trying to take things further, but I kept brushing him off. Eventually, I gave in and one thing led to another.

I remember as he was undressing me, he said, 'I don't remember you being this skinny. I love skinny girls and you are perfect for me.' I remember laughing inside and secretly thinking I wasn't that skinny the first time he had seen me: the hours and hours in the gym had paid off. I was really excited because I honestly thought it was the start of a romance, but for him it was obviously just something he did all the time. There was me expecting him to call and ask me out but I didn't realise it didn't work like that. Calum just wanted sex and that was pretty much it. He would text me when he was on a night out and ask me to go back to his, or we'd bump into each other in a club and I'd end up going back with him.

I was still thinking this was the start of a relationship. I'd been with Matthew for seven years, so this was all new to me. I didn't realise what lengths guys will go to just to get you into bed. I mean, I thought he was going to paint the spare room pink but, really, he was just a big fat love rat.

We carried on like that for a month or so, but there were never any proper dates. I was so very naive. I'd been with Matthew for so long that I was totally inexperienced when it came to men. I didn't get how it worked for blokes like Calum, and that romance wasn't really on the cards, never mind a relationship.

Things with Calum completely fizzled out. The texts and calls pretty much stopped, and things cooled off. So I guess that was it – what I thought could have been the start of a relationship ended pretty much over night.

My dalliance with Calum gave me my first insight into what the men mixing in these circles are like. I'd never met anyone like that before. Although it had been fun and exciting, and had seemed to be glamorous at the time, it wasn't the best start to my fabulous single life.

Through all this, I decided to keep up my weight loss as all the other girls on the scene were really skinny. I virtually stopped eating. In the morning, I would have a black coffee while Mady had her breakfast. I remember being hungry, but I was determined. I would take Mady to the crèche at the gym and then do a really big workout. I used to feel really dizzy and faint, but I just sipped water to get me through it. Afterwards, I would sit in the gym car park and eat a tin of mackerel in tomato sauce and a banana. That would be it for the whole day. I soon went down to a size 6, and, although permanently exhausted, I loved the feeling of being that thin. I didn't realise at the time that this was a totally unhealthy way to live.

I was totally obsessed with fashion as well, and I was determined to look different to everyone else so I would stand out. I'd always had a wacky, unconventional dress sense – I never wanted to wear what everyone else was wearing, I wanted to be ahead of the fashions.

I started going out more and more, and I realised that, actually, the weekends in central London weren't the best nights to go out, as most of Essex would be there; the cool crowd went out on a Wednesday. So, I would get my Nanny

Linda to babysit and started going out on a Wednesday night. Mady would go to bed at 8pm at mine and I would start getting ready.

One week, I went to a Halloween party at Movida with Helen and was approached by an American guy. He explained he recognised me from being out with Calum, who was a very good friend of his. We got chatting and he seemed really nice – as a friend rather than anything else – and he told me he was a club promoter. He gave me his number and invited me to boxer David Haye's after party the following weekend. I couldn't wait!

The party was on 24 November 2007 and I had no idea this was to be the night when I would meet the love of my life.

I had invited my cousin Frankie and her friend Danielle. They were really excited. I'd made myself a top that was really tight and tucked it into leather-look jeans. I was tiny by this point, but I still didn't think I was skinny enough. The party was at a really trendy club called 5 Cavendish Square, which is just off Oxford Street and I thought it was really cool. When we arrived, it was already packed. There were loads of really glam people there and the music was brilliant. I was driving so I wasn't drinking, but Frankie and Danielle were so excited that they ended up getting really drunk.

Anyway, I went over to say hi to my club promoter friend and to thank him for inviting me and he was chatting to this really petite, beautiful girl. He introduced me to her – her name was Ellie and she was from Manchester. He told me that she was Simon Webbe's PA, so I told her all about that bizarre day when Simon had stopped me on the street and given me his card. I said that I regretted turning down such a great opportunity. We got chatting and we just got on really well. Although she was from Manchester, she had moved to London because she worked for Simon and she was living in Buckhurst Hill, really near me.

She told me she had just split from her boyfriend and she was lonely because all her friends were back in Manchester, but, as her job was being Simon's PA, she had to stay in Essex. We got on really well and instantly became friends. Ellie is now one of my best friends. Over the past five years, she has been a real friend to me and I often wonder how I would have coped without her. It sounds corny but she has been my rock.

After a few hours at 5 Cavendish Square, people started leaving and the party was dying down, so Frankie, Danielle and me headed to Movida. We went straight into the VIP area and, while I was sober, Frankie must have drunk loads by this point and she was absolutely hammered. She had managed to lose her shoes – God knows how – and I was thinking I really needed to get her out of there and get her home.

The next thing, I looked up and saw a man standing on the edge of the VIP area, who I hadn't noticed before. He was wearing black trousers and a black shirt, with an orange Hermès belt and an orange cashmere jumper placed carefully over his shoulders. A black granddad cap finished his look. My very first thought was he looked very stylish. I couldn't help wondering who he was because I'd never seen a man wearing an orange jumper in a club before! Something about him seemed mysterious and attractive all at the same time. I thought he was foreign as he was tall, dark and handsome.

I caught his eye, and he pointed and beckoned me over. Normally, if a man had tried to do that, I would have blanked him, but something about this man intrigued me. As soon as he spoke, it shocked me: he had a cockney accent. That sparked an instant conversation. He was funny, confident and clean-cut. It was obvious he was a real gentleman, generous and polite with a slight arrogance, which I loved!

Close up, he was really good-looking, with short dark hair, dark eyes and a contagious smile. He was also the perfect height: taller than me, with a strong compact build. He told me he was from north London, but he didn't give much else away. By this point, Frankie was extremely drunk and I could see the doormen were keeping a close eye on her. I decided I'd better sort Frankie out, so I went over to her and lost this handsome stranger in the crowd. We got our things together and made our way to the exit. It took a while as Danielle and me had to hold Frankie up. The three of us were all laughing and trying to act as if Frankie wasn't drunk. As I looked up, there was the handsome stranger again, standing in front of me and talking on his phone; I carried on walking.

Once we were outside the club, I searched through my handbag, otherwise known as the bomb, for my car keys. Not an easy task, as it was packed with stuff. He must have been watching because, when I found my keys, he asked if I was driving. I told him I was, and he said, 'You can drive my car.' I just laughed but he got his car keys out of his pocket and pressed the button to unlock his car. As he did so, I noticed a flash brand-new black sports car parked next to us. My answer was: 'I can't drive that!' It was a big sports car and I had only been driving for a few years.

He invited us to an after party and we accepted, as I was so intrigued by who he was and what he was about. We all piled into his sports car and he took us to the Soho Hotel, just a few streets away. When we walked in, the staff were saying hello to him – they obviously knew him – and we went into a private bar area downstairs, and he got us all food and more drinks.

By this time, Frankie and Danielle were totally smashed and Danielle was sick everywhere – right in the middle of the hotel bar area. My handsome stranger was standing right next to her but he didn't seem that bothered by it. I told him I thought it was time we left and asked him to take me to the toilets, as I didn't know where they were (I wanted to go for a wee before I drove the girls home). He showed me to the toilet and then followed me in. I laughed and asked what he was doing as he was so forward, but not in a sleazy way. He simply said, 'Taking you to the toilet, like you asked me to.'

I put my bag down on the sink area, asked him to look after it and then went into the toilet cubicle. When I came out, he was there waiting. It was the early hours and no one was around so we were finally alone. I opened my trusty bomb and, as usual, the contents exploded all over the place. He couldn't believe the stuff I had in there and was laughing at it all – especially the fake-tan mitt – and then, when I told him it was called the bomb, he looked at me in amusement. I thought he seemed really nice but I couldn't figure him out. He seemed different to the other guys I'd met and I was even more intrigued.

I asked him to drive me back to my car to collect it and he said that was fine. I joked that I didn't actually know how to get back to Essex – I just used to make it up as I went along and I always found my way back in the end! After asking for my address, he put it in his Sat Nav. He told me he would make sure I got home OK and I could follow him in my car.

Next thing I knew, we were going in the wrong direction to my car and I realised we were on our way to Essex. 'What are you doing?' I asked, and he said, 'Don't worry, we'll just get your car in the morning.' I panicked and said I needed my car as I had to take Mady to nursery in the morning; also, I couldn't leave my cousin and friend in a hotel in the middle of London, so we turned back, got my car, collected the girls and headed home with me following him.

I dropped Frankie and Danielle off and then, when we got to mine, he parked his car and got out. It had been a long drive, it was the weekend and Mady was with her grandparents, so I invited him into the house. He asked if I had anything to drink, so I got a bottle of vodka out and we sat up chatting and drinking until it was broad daylight outside.

Eventually, I told him that I had to get to bed because I needed to be up as it was my Nanny Daisy's 99th birthday that day and we were all going to visit her in the old people's home. But he still didn't leave: he just walked upstairs, took all his clothes off apart from his pants and climbed into my bed. I found it funny – I couldn't believe how confident he was – so I put my pyjamas on and got into bed as well.

We had a kiss but nothing else happened and then he fell

asleep. He started snoring in minutes and I lay there, thinking, 'Who is this man snoring my entire house down?'

It might sound weird that I invited him back to my house just hours after I had met him, but for some reason he just seemed trustworthy. I know he could have been anyone but it just instantly felt right. I guess, looking back, I trusted him before I should have, but he just had that effect on me.

When we woke up, I realised I was going to be late to go and see my Nanny Daisy so I told him he'd have to go – but, before he left, he asked for my number.

Later that day, he rang me and invited me out to a concert that night. I was knackered but he was really persistent so I said I would go. My cousin Frankie offered to babysit, so, even though I was exhausted, I got all glammed up and sat waiting for him. The time ticked by, but he didn't come – he had called a few times to explain that he was having a nightmare and was running late. He offered to get someone to pick me up but I refused, saying, 'You either come and get me or I'm not coming!' I wasn't being a diva but I had decided that after Calum I would not be messed around again, and I was starting as I meant to go on. Even though I really wanted to see him, I felt I must be strong this time.

I had high hopes for him so I decided I had to play this one by the rulebook. After a few phone calls, I got fed up and told him to leave it, which he did.

In the end, I went to bed, and the next thing I was woken by my phone ringing. I told him I was in bed asleep, but he just said, 'I need to talk to you. I'm on the way to your house.' It was the middle of the night but he said he didn't care. So I got up, made sure my make-up looked OK and waited. But he never came.

How had I let this happen? He had let me down twice in one night, and I'd had enough of these men making me promises and then letting me down.

It was over it before it had even started – or so I thought.

CHAPTER NINE

Love of My Life

After he had let me down twice, I assumed it was all over with the mystery man. Little did I know it was just the beginning; I thought he was good-looking and mysterious that first night when I met him in Movida, but I had no idea only weeks later I would fall head over heels in love. I can honestly say he's the love of my life, and always will be.

It all started the morning after he stood me up twice in one day. He rang and asked me for another chance. I told him no, but he wouldn't give up. Eventually, I gave in and he said he would pick me up to take me out for dinner a few days later on the Friday (I had to spend time with Mady and she would be with her grandparents then). By this time, I wasn't getting my hopes up and was half-expecting him not to turn up.

In between him standing me up and our date, Ellie (Simon

Webbe's PA, who I'd met earlier on that same night) called for a chat and I invited her round for a cup of tea. I told her everything that had happened on my mad few days after I left her at David Haye's after party and about the date planned for that Friday. After chatting for a while, I also explained that I wanted to do glamour modelling – I'd realised by this point that I wasn't going to be a fashion model, so I thought I would try glamour instead. Ellie said she knew a lot of people in the industry after working as Simon's PA for the past ten years.

She told me she knew an agent and organised a meeting for me on the following Saturday, the day after my date. The agent turned out to be Dave Read, Calum Best's manager, who I'd met all those months earlier. I was really grateful for Ellie's help and felt like things were coming together.

So Friday came and I dropped Mady at her grandparents' as usual and my thoughts turned to my date that night. It was our first official date. He said he would pick me up and this time he did turn up. As I was half-expecting him to let me down, I didn't rush to get ready and do my normal routine, so when he did turn up I was in a real rush!

From the minute I got into his car, he proved he was different to all the other men I had met. He played a song I'd never heard before with the volume turned right up and I remember thinking, 'What a mad song!' It was 'You Are My Starship' by a group called Dazz Band. It's a love song and from that moment on – in my head at least – he became known as 'Mr Starship'.

He asked which of the nearby restaurants were nice to go and eat. It was a bit late and I wasn't sure where we would get in, so I suggested the Miller and Carter Steakhouse on the outskirts of Chigwell because I knew they served until quite late. We drove out there and, when we walked in, I realised just how confident he was. He marched straight up to the waiter and told him where we wanted to sit; he just seemed so in control. He chose a table meant for four people, with a bench for two people one side and then two chairs opposite. I sat down at the far end of the bench and then, instead of sitting opposite me, like a normal person, he slid along the bench and sat right next to me. I told him people were looking at us because it was weird to be sitting in a line, but he didn't care. He simply said, 'We're not in an interview – I want to sit next to you.'

I ordered a salad because I didn't want to eat a heavy meal. He questioned my choice as we were in a steakhouse, but I explained I had a meeting the following day with an agent who looks after celebrities and glamour models. I told him I was considering doing glamour modelling, which I don't think he was too impressed about.

When our food arrived, he said, 'I can't take your salad seriously. Come on, you're eating some of mine.' He then tried to force-feed me his steak and, when I said no, he lifted the fork, did a plane noise as loud as a car horn and moved the fork towards my mouth – like you would with a small child. I panicked as people were already staring at us because of his choice of seating arrangement and now he was drawing even more attention to us. I reluctantly ate it to save my embarrassment. It immediately broke the ice and I felt comfortable and able to be myself. It proved he was being himself, so I let my guard down and we enjoyed our dinner.

As the evening went on, something just really clicked between us. I was nervous so I had a few drinks and felt really relaxed around him. He was good-looking and funny, and there was a definite spark there. I really fancied him.

When the waiter came over to ask if we wanted dessert, I opened my mouth to say no but, before I had the chance, he just cut in and said, 'Yes, she does. She'll have the banoffee pie.'

'I can't believe you have just ordered a pudding for me. I don't want one!'

'Tough, we're going to share it.'

So, he basically force-fed me banoffee pie! I guess maybe he thought I needed feeding up – which I did.

The night flew by and we talked about anything and every-thing, and laughed a lot. By the time we finished eating, we were the last people in the whole restaurant but I didn't want the evening to end. I remember looking at his profile and thinking, 'I'm going to marry this man.'

As we walked out into the car park, he spotted a grassy hill and dared me to roll down it. Now I never turn down a dare so I said I would, even though I was wearing nice clothes and it was all muddy. And I would have done it, too, but he stopped me just before I did!

We went back to mine and I thought in my head, 'I am not going to sleep with this man' – I could tell he was special and I wanted to wait. He started kissing me and, before I knew it, my plans went out the window. I was so lost in the magic of the evening that I gave into temptation and we spent the night together.

From that point on, my life would forever change. After just one date, he had knocked me off my feet. I was completely head over heels: he was so funny and handsome, and just formal and old-fashioned in a chivalrous kind of way, which was totally different to any of the guys I'd been out with before.

The morning after that first official date, I woke up feeling really excited. Not only did I have the man of my dreams asleep in my bed, but it was also the day of my meeting with Dave Read. I was determined not to be late so I'd planned to drive and set off in plenty of time. As I didn't have a Sat Nav, Mr Starship offered to drive ahead and I would follow behind.

Dave Read's office was in Islington and we set off towards north London. After a while, I realised we were heading for east rather than north London because I knew that area so well – we were right near my Nanny Daisy's. So I rang him and said, 'Why are we in east London when we are meant to be going to Islington?' I couldn't believe his reply – 'I want to stop off and get some pie and mash.' I was speechless. He had taken me on a massive detour that would potentially make me late for an important meeting, all because he fancied pie and mash at nine o'clock in the morning!

But that's just Mr Starship for you – he fancied pie and mash, and so that's what he had. He just does whatever he wants, whenever he wants. He asked if I wanted some and I just looked at him as if he was mad, but he didn't notice and just tucked in.

We eventually made it to Dave Read's office and luckily we weren't late, despite the pie and mash detour. Mr Starship kissed me goodbye and left me there. I was already desperate to see him again, but first I had to focus on my potentially life-changing meeting.

I was so nervous my legs felt like jelly, but Dave was really nice and he seemed to really like me. I told him I was planning to have a boob job and he said it wasn't necessary for me to have them done. But by this point I had made up my mind 100 per cent. I couldn't stand my tiny boobs and there was no way I was posing topless unless they were much bigger, so I told him I was definitely getting them done and he was happy with that. He told me all about modelling and I was really excited.

I went home and booked my boob job for the following January – just a month away – and Dave told me I could have a test shoot done six weeks after the operation. I couldn't wait. Things were finally looking up: I'd met Mr Starship and I was taking the first steps to achieve my ambition of becoming a glamour model. I'd arranged to have my boob job in Belgium because it was a lot cheaper to have the operation over there. A friend had had hers done over there and had told me how great it was. I still had savings left and I planned to use those – I thought it would be an investment for my career.

My blossoming romance with Mr Starship was amazing. We started spending every free moment we had together. I had really fallen for him and we became inseparable. I stopped going out, started playing 'wifey' and he would stay over at mine almost every night. I fell so deeply in love; I just knew he was The One.

He asked me to move in with him, but I felt it was too soon as I had Mady and was scared to move to London with her. I have regretted saying no ever since. We talked about marriage, children, everything. I remember thinking, 'This is why I've been through so much shit, because I would meet him, the man of my dreams, and live happily ever after.'

As time went on, I began to find more things I loved about him: his morals, his old-fashioned values. I loved the sound of his voice and the way he would sing to me. He was perfect down to every last detail. I'd never felt like this before, ever.

But there was one downside to my otherwise perfect new romance – I was putting on weight. I started cooking meals for Mr Starship, which meant I had to eat with him. I couldn't exactly make him a meal and then not eat it. He used to take me out to eat all the time as well, so I was eating more than I had done for years. My stomach started getting bigger and I hated it. I felt constantly bloated and I became constipated – I guess, because my body wasn't used to digesting so much food, it couldn't handle it.

The constipation and bloating got so bad that I went to the doctor and they told me to change my diet and gave me some advice. He told me to eat more fibre and lots of fruit and vegetables but the diet didn't really help, and I was still in pain from the bloating. I went back to the doctor but they just fobbed me off again. In the end, it got so bad I went to see a private doctor and told him all about the bloating and constipation. He said he thought I had a blockage and so he gave me a prescription for this special laxative that is given to people before they have an operation to get rid of everything in their stomachs.

The new laxative was the answer to my prayers! Literally everything came out, and all of a sudden I wasn't bloated and uncomfortable any more. But, as soon as I ate anything, I would get bloated again. So I went back to my normal GP and asked if they could give me the same strong stuff, and they did, but they said I couldn't keep having it because it's not meant to be used often. The problem didn't go away and I realised it wasn't a prescription drug so I could buy it over the counter and I started to take it all the time.

After a while, I realised I couldn't carry on because through taking laxatives I was losing bowel control, but, every time I ate, I would feel bloated again. I was stuck in a vicious circle: I had to stop taking the laxatives but I couldn't starve myself as before because Mr Starship would notice.

Things got worse. I got to the point where I couldn't stand having anything in my belly, so I would make myself sick. I'd always been able to stick my fingers down my throat if I was too drunk on a night out, so I knew I could do it, but sometimes if I'd eaten a big meal it would take ages. I started drinking loads of water before I ate anything as that made it much easier to puke up afterwards.

I became good at hiding it, but I was looking awful. I looked ill – I was really skinny, with big, bulgy eyes. Because Mr Starship was spending so much time at mine, it became more and more difficult to keep it from him. He noticed that I kept disappearing after meals and he began to suspect something. I felt so close to him that I decided to confide in him that I was bulimic. He was really understanding but afterwards it became even more difficult to make myself sick because he knew the signs and was watching me.

But I couldn't stop. I would try not to make myself sick when he was around so that he was less likely to suspect. I guess he thought I was getting over it, but I wasn't – I was just getting more devious.

I did my best to put my bulimia to the back of my mind and instead concentrated on the positives: I was with the man of my dreams, it was nearly Christmas and I was getting really excited about my boob job in January. Everything was so perfect until Matthew put a spanner in the works. He had found out about me and Mr Starship and he was insanely jealous. I had been single since we split in the spring of that year – apart from my short-lived fling with Calum – and he couldn't handle the thought of me moving on and having a new man.

He was so jealous that he took our lovely car and refused to give it back. I was really annoyed; I needed a car to get me and Mady around.

I then realised that my money was running out. The savings I'd been living on from the sale of the house had come to an end and there was literally nothing left. Matthew stopped giving me any money for Mady and with no job I was completely skint. Once I'd paid for Christmas presents, the money was gone. I had just enough left to pay for my boob job and not a penny more.

I couldn't live without a car. I needed to buy one as soon as possible, so I asked my dad for advice on a second-hand car. I explained that Matthew had taken our car and he said he would see what he could do. He rang me back later that day and said I was in luck: a friend of his was getting rid of his car and had offered it to my dad, really cheap. Dad was brilliant. 'Save your money, I'll get it for you,' he said. Luckily for me, it was an automatic because I couldn't drive anything else – I only had an automatic licence.

'Thanks, Dad,' I said, 'I really appreciate it.' Once again, my amazing dad had come to the rescue. He told me it was a Toyota Corolla. I had no idea what it looked like – I was just grateful to have a car again.

Later that same day, his friend turned up at my house in it and I suddenly regretted saying thanks. It was the ugliest car I had ever seen, it was grey and a proper old banger – the most un-cool car I'd ever laid eyes on! It was a K-reg, which meant it was about 15 years old and was falling apart. One of the lights at the front was missing and had been patched up with a mineral water bottle with some gaffer tape round it. I swear it was hideous!

But even the seriously un-cool car didn't dampen my spirits. I was so excited about Christmas. I had always loved Christmas ever since I was a little girl, and me and Auntie Sylv would spend ages decorating the tree and then she'd make a real fuss of me with loads of presents. I wanted to make it just as special for Mady, so I went all out and dipped into my savings. I also wanted my first Christmas with Mr Starship to be special. My only problem was what to buy the man who has everything, so I really splashed out.

Mr Starship was due to come to mine on Christmas Day. I was determined that it would be perfect. He came round on

Christmas Eve and gave me the money to go out and buy the food for the next day. I wouldn't have accepted it as I like to pay my own way, but I had spent so much on presents I was short by this point. Mr Starship said he had some errands to run, but he would be back later that night. I didn't mind as I still had a lot of organising to do and I was so excited. I went out and bought all the food, and I just couldn't wait to spend the day with the love of my life. We'd only been together a month, but that didn't matter – I was totally smitten. It got later and later, but I just presumed he was taking presents to his family or out having a drink, as most men do on Christmas Eve.

On Christmas morning, Mady woke me up all excited and it hit me that Mr Starship hadn't come home. I was worried sick but had to put on a brave face and pretend I wasn't upset for Mady's sake. Mady and me got up and tore open our presents. I rang Mr Starship and he explained one of his friends had had trouble the night before and he was helping him. As soon as I heard his voice and realised he was still alive, I was fuming. All the worry in my head turned to anger. He asked what time dinner would be ready and I said, 'Don't you dare come over here!' In my eyes, he had ruined our first Christmas. I then started making the dinner I had bought. The deal with Matthew was that I would have Mady on Christmas Day and then he and his parents would have her on Boxing Day, and that's still the same arrangement now.

Mr Starship didn't turn up. My dad rang to wish Mady and me a Happy Christmas and I couldn't admit my man had stood us up on Christmas Day so I pretended everything was fine. If I'd told him it was just Mady and me, he would have made me go over to his house, but I was far too upset. My perfect day was ruined.

After Mady had her dinner and Christmas pudding, I put her down for a sleep and decided to have a glass of mulled wine. After half a glass, I found myself reaching for my mobile and ringing Mr Starship. He answered with a grumpy tone and I asked him where he was. He said he was at his mum's. I asked if he had eaten yet and he said he hadn't. I explained that I'd made his dinner and wanted him to come round as I missed him. I was relieved when he said he'd come over.

I always knew when Mr Starship was pulling up at my house – his sports car was so loud! It would immediately set the butterflies off and I would run around like a mad woman, doing final hair and make-up checks and making sure my house was perfect. He would always greet me at the door with a soft passionate kiss, like something from a romantic movie. As soon as I saw him, I forgave him. We managed to eat our dinner and Mady woke up and joined us. We all pulled the crackers and had party hats on. It was the perfect end to what had started off as a nightmare day.

After dinner, Mr Starship went to his car and brought in presents for Mady and me. He had bought the most beautiful and thoughtful gifts, including an outfit and shoes for me to wear on Boxing Day. I was really touched that he had gone out and bought them all, and even wrapped them up himself. We had a romantic night, just the two of us after Mady had gone to bed, and later I went to bed, feeling really content and happy.

On Boxing Day, Mady was picked up by her grandparents, as she was going to be spending the day with them and her dad at their house. Mr Starship and me decided we would go out that evening. Some of the girls from the previous May in Marbella were going to a do at Woolston Manor Golf and Country Club. I hadn't seen them for a few weeks because I was so loved up with Mr Starship and they were desperate to meet him. He loves a party, so we were both looking forward to it. I put on the designer dress he had bought me, but it didn't fit. As I was so skinny, it was too big and I was gutted. He said I could exchange it, but I never did because he had bought it for me and it was so special. I put on another dress and my new shoes, and off we went.

I was so proud that Mr Starship was out with me and he was a big hit with all my friends as he was so charming. After all the stress of him being late and the worry about Christmas being perfect, I ended up getting really drunk. I was downing drinks and I ended up being sick all over my shoes he had bought me for Christmas. How glamorous!

We were meant to be going into central London after the golf club, but Mr Starship realised he needed to get me home and so we went to leave. The bouncer on the door knew my dad and my uncle Don, and as we were trying to leave he stopped us. He could see how drunk I was, and he obviously thought Mr Starship had just met me and was worried he was about to take advantage of me in that state. He grabbed Mr Starship and said, 'Who are you?'

I was trying to tell him he was my boyfriend and I remember slurring, 'He's the love of my life!' Eventually, they let us leave.

As soon as he woke up the following morning, Mr Starship announced he had to go. He told me he was going up north and it was important, but I was fuming and started having a go at him. He hadn't told me he was leaving and I didn't want him to go. We'd planned a big night for New Year's Eve, which I was really looking forward to; he promised me he would be back. I remember him saying, 'I won't let you down.'

He left and we spoke on the phone each day. Every day, he would tell me he would be back the next day but he never came. New Year's Eve arrived and he still hadn't come. I was devastated and I missed him so much. I had promised my old school friend Helen that she could come out with us as she hadn't made plans, and then we were left with nothing to do.

It got to 3pm and he still wasn't back and I realised there was no way he would be back in time. By this time, I was angry so I decided there was no way Helen and me were sitting in on New Year's Eve. I rang the manager of Movida and told him we'd been let down and he said we could go there.

As soon as I put the phone down, it rang: Mr Starship. I was moody with him and told him I'd made plans. I explained to him that there was no way he would be back in time. He argued that he wouldn't have let me down. By this point, he was annoyed and just told me to enjoy my night with Helen and then put the phone down.

He probably had no intention of coming back, but me saying I'd made plans gave him the opportunity to turn it all round on me. I kept trying to ring him back, but he blanked me. After that, I just wanted to stay in, but I couldn't let Helen down and so off we went to Movida. I was determined to try to enjoy myself.

It had been a pretty eventful year, what with splitting with Matthew and starting my glamorous new single life. I'd had plenty of ups and downs but I wanted the New Year to be the start of a whole new era. I was having my long-awaited boob job in a few weeks' time, going for my first ever glamour-modelling shoot, and had met the love of my life. But the path of true love wasn't exactly running smoothly.

I thought he would at least call me but midnight came and went with no text or phone call from Mr Starship and so I saw the New Year in, crying in the middle of Movida. I loved him and was so frightened of losing him. It wasn't the great start to 2008 I was hoping for, and so looking forward to.

Mr Starship blanked me for several days after that. Over the years, this has become a regular pattern. We'll have a row and he'll ignore me for days and then all of a sudden he'll pop up again, all forgotten and go back to the way things were. In the middle of an argument while I'm ranting and raving, he'll simply say, 'I'm not angry, I'm just disappointed' – it's always the same phrase and I make fun of him when he says it now – and then he just blanks me. I'll be ringing and texting him like a nutter and he'll just ignore me until he's ready to speak to me again.

About a week later, Mr Starship popped back up. Even though I was so angry and felt let down, as soon as I saw his name flash up on my phone I couldn't help myself – I answered the call. My stomach was doing somersaults, but, as soon as I heard his voice, all of my hurt and disappointment drifted away. He made me laugh within seconds, singing one of our songs loudly. He can't sing but has a very distinctive voice, which I love. We made plans on the phone, and agreed that he would stay with me every night of that week. I loved it when he stayed the night with me. The plan sounded perfect.

I'd often fall asleep waiting for him on the sofa and be woken by him gently tapping on the window. I'd instantly smile and no matter how late he was, he'd always turn up with chocolate or something sweet and put it on the stair case in the hall. Some nights I'd drive over to his house and he would always really look after me by making me dinner and cups of tea and making sure he had all my favourite things stocked up. We would get cosy on the sofa and watch black and white movies together! We'd be so content that one of us would always doze off, normally him snoring, but I didn't mind! Sometimes I'd lie awake and watch him sleep, taking in every last detail of his face. I was so deeply, uncontrollably in love.

One night, he randomly suggested we go out for a walk at 2am, and reluctantly I changed heels for UGG boots and ventured outside with him. I was slightly bemused but happily walked arm in arm with my beautiful prince. We were chatting and for the first time Mr Starship opened up about his own life. He told me about his upbringing and in the end we walked so far and talked for so long we ended up lost! It didn't matter where we were or where we went I just loved being with him. He has done lots of mad, random things like this for almost a year and I guess that, apart from having so much charm and being so handsome, I felt so deeply in love with him that I couldn't hold a grudge. So, even though we had cleared the air, I tried to focus on my impending boob job and not on Mr Starship. When I told my dad that I was going to have my boobs done, he wasn't happy. His response was: 'What are you doing that for?' But I told him I had made my decision and he accepted it because he could see my mind was made up.

It annoys me when people have a go at me about having plastic surgery – I was 26 when I had my boob job. I would never advise anyone having surgery younger than that. I was old enough to know what I wanted and I made my own decision. A lot of the girls on *TOWIE* had theirs done when they were much younger.

By this time, my battle with food was raging on. Struggling to keep my bulimia under control, I was too weak to go to the gym. I got more and more skinny but I didn't care – my boob job would change it all.

I told Mr Starship I was off to Belgium to have my boobs done and he said he would come with me. I really wanted him by my side because I was so nervous, so I was really happy about that. But I also knew how unreliable he was, and I didn't believe he would actually come.

I packed my case and had just set off for St Pancras station, where I was catching the Eurostar, when he rang and told me he would be there waiting for me. I still didn't believe him, so when I got there I was prepared to be disappointed. As I walked out on to the station concourse, he rang me again and told me he was there. I looked over and there he was, holding a single rose wrapped in cellophane and a teddy – I was so happy he was coming with me!

We caught the Eurostar and spent the journey playing cards. Mr Starship is really competitive and it made me laugh that he'd get so annoyed when he didn't win.

When we arrived in Brussels, Mr Starship sorted everything. He had ordered a cab and booked a really nice hotel, not far from the clinic. We checked in and he gave me a box of my favourite Godiva chocolates. He lay down and had a sleep. I lay next to him, eating my chocolates and thinking how lucky I was, and how much I loved him.

My operation was booked for the following day so Mr Starship said he was taking me out for dinner. I told him I wasn't allowed to drink because of the op, but as usual he just went ahead and kept ordering me beers. Apparently, it's Belgian tradition to drink beer and they had one called Blonde, so how could I say no? I hadn't realised that Belgian beer is much stronger than the beer at home and before long I was drunk. It was nearly the end of the night and, after a long meal, I noticed the restaurant had cleared. All the waiters were standing there with their arms crossed, waiting for us to leave. As usual, Mr Starship was completely oblivious and, as a romantic song came on, he asked me to have a slow dance. 'Are you kidding me?' was my response. He then stood up, so I followed and he held me in his arms. Just as I was thinking how romantic it was, the annoyed waiters switched the music off. Both of us found it hilarious and laughed the place down. We got the bill and left.

We started walking back to the hotel and my shoes were killing me so I took them off. Mr Starship got in a mood. He doesn't like things like that – he thinks it's common – so he stormed off ahead. When I finally hobbled up to the front of the hotel, he was waiting outside with a bellboy trolley. He lifted me up, put me on the trolley like a suitcase and wheeled me through the reception and into the bar.

He stood at the bar, totally straight-faced with me next to him on the trolley and tried to order a drink, but unsurprisingly the barman wouldn't serve him. So, he pushed me and the trolley out of the bar, back across the foyer and into the lift. I was laughing, everyone was staring at us, but he just didn't care. He pushed me all the way to our hotel-room door and carried me into bed.

When I woke up the next morning, I'd forgotten all about it until I walked out of the room and saw the trolley in the corridor!

On the morning of the operation, I was so nervous I felt really sick. I was excited because I thought it would change my life but at the same time I was shitting myself.

I had chosen to have my operation at the Elyzea clinic in Brussels, the same clinic my friend had recommended. She had told me how nice and clean it was. It was also so much cheaper than having it done in the UK, about half the price. Since my op, I have recommended it to loads of other people and they have been really pleased with it too.

The clinic was about 20 minutes from our hotel and, when we arrived, I was pleased to see it was just as my friend had described it: everything was white. We went to have a chat with the consultant and I made sure not to mention that I had been drinking the previous night. The first thing he asked was how big I wanted to go.

'As big as possible,' was my instant reply.

But Mr Starship wasn't impressed. 'No, not too big.'

Then the surgeon asked if I wanted to go behind the muscle or in front of the muscle. 'In front,' I said (that way, they would be bigger). Again, Mr Starship disagreed. In the end, we reached a compromise: I got the big, round implants I wanted, but I would have them behind the muscle. This would take me from an empty B-cup to a DD.

I was shown to my room, where I changed into the hospital gown. Essex through and through, I had all my make-up with me and I even wore my false eyelashes for the operation. There was no way I was letting Mr Starship see me without my make-up on!

I remember him kissing me before I was wheeled down to the operating theatre and then the next thing I was lying in bed after the op. The first thing I did was look down at my boobs. They looked massive! I was in agony – it felt like someone was sitting on my chest.

I then looked over and saw Mr Starship, and everything was OK again. I was really emotional because of the operation and the anaesthetic. I kept crying and telling him I loved him and he was brilliant – he'd even gone out and bought me a fresh croissant, which he fed to me piece by piece. I couldn't lift my arms properly and he even tried his best to do my hair and make-up for me before I left the hospital but I ended up looking like a clown!

When I was allowed to check out later that day, Mr Starship announced he was starving. We walked past a local restaurant and he said, 'This will do, let's go in here.' We walked in and it was packed. It was as if there was a private function or something going on; everyone seemed to know each other and they were all Belgian. The owner was going round filling everyone's glasses up, and there was us, right in the middle of them. I said, 'Let's go somewhere else,' but Mr Starship refused. Typical, I thought. I felt awkward but he didn't care, so we stayed. Everyone was staring at us but Mr Starship doesn't even notice stuff like that. They must have wondered what on earth we were doing there. I'd just come out of hospital and was off the planet – I could barely lift my arms. I looked like a crack addict!

Later that night, we headed back to the UK, again on the Eurostar, and I was really excited about my topless photoshoot. I loved my new boobs – they were big and round, and I was really happy with them. Dave Read had booked me a shoot with a female photographer who worked for a company called Popstars, one of the country's biggest glamour photo agencies. She was so lovely and, although I was really nervous, she put me totally at ease. It felt weird being there in front of the camera with just a pair of knickers on but my new boobs gave me confidence. Soon my nerves turned into excitement and I enjoyed the experience.

A few weeks later, I went back to see Dave Read with the pictures that Popstars had taken and he seemed positive about them. He said he could get me work and he sent the shots off to loads of magazines. He then suggested that I should do another, more sexy shoot now I was feeling a bit more confident and I agreed.

So, off I went for a second photoshoot with a photographer called Mark Barnfield, who had his own studio in north London. He was really nice and this time I stripped naked and we did implied nude pictures – although I was naked, you couldn't see anything in the pictures.

I was really positive about the whole thing and I thought this would be the start of my glamour-modelling career. Looking back now, it was never going to happen. I was far too skinny; there was no way anyone was going to buy those pictures with me looking skin and bone. I wish Dave Read had been more honest with me at the time and told me that it wasn't going to work out rather than getting my hopes up. I was too skinny, but I just couldn't see it at the time. I had an eating disorder and I was ill.

I still believed I would make money from glamour modelling but, in the meantime, I was totally skint. I had spent the last of my savings on my boob job, thinking it was an investment for my modelling career. Now I needed cash desperately: I had rent to pay and a child to look after. My friend Ellie had moved out of her place in Buckhurst Hill and was desperate for somewhere to live, so I asked her to move in with me. We'd been great friends since we first met, she was lonely and I thought it would be nice for me to have some adult company. My little house had two downstairs rooms and we converted one of them into a bedroom for Ellie, so that Mady and me still had our own rooms upstairs. Best of all, Ellie paid half the rent, which meant I could just about manage financially. I didn't want to admit to Mr Starship how skint I was – I wanted to try to cope on my own.

Not long after I'd had my boob job, my Nanny Daisy died. It was a really sad time for the whole family. Although she was 99 and had been poorly for a few years, it was awful for the family because it brought back memories of Auntie Tina's death six years earlier. It was really hard. Another funeral and we had lost another special member of our family. It was difficult for us all, but especially hard for my Nanny Linda: she'd lost her daughter and now she'd lost her mum.

At the funeral, we were crying for Auntie Tina as much as we were for Nanny Daisy. Nanny Daisy was 99 and she'd had a really long life so, although it was sad, at the same time, we could accept it. We all knew she had wanted to die for the last few years when her health started deteriorating. She used to say, 'What am I still doing here?' and I would always tell her that she had to hang on until she was 100 so she could get her telegram from the Queen. She died not long after she had turned 99, so she never did get that telegram.

She was such a strong woman – she had remained in her own flat until she was 97 and, apart from being pretty deaf, she was totally with it. You just had to shout when you went round there! She'd had a hip replacement at the age of 95 and the doctors warned us that she might not make it through the operation, but she was tough as old boots.

When she got to 97, she kept falling over and hurting

herself, so she had to go into a home. She was a proud woman and she didn't want to leave her flat where she'd lived all her life, but there was no choice. Once she got into the home, she deteriorated really quickly – it was really sad. She started getting dementia and, even though her husband had died when he was young, she kept thinking he was still alive. In the end, she just died of old age; her body simply gave up and she passed away peacefully.

All of a sudden, it was May again and a year since my trip to Marbella. I had promised myself 12 months earlier that I would be back the following year and that I would have had a boob job and sorted my image out, and now I had. So, I planned my Bank Holiday trip to give myself something to look forward to.

My dad's friend lived in Marbella and offered to help me out. He sorted me a hotel so I only had to scrape together enough money for a flight. Ellie and I only had 200 Euros between us for the whole weekend but we both knew a lot of people from London who were promoting the parties out there. They said we could join their tables, meaning we had free drinks a lot of the time.

I had made a pact with myself that I would never again feel like I'd done the previous year when I felt so inferior to all the other girls. This time I went back to the same Champagne Spray Party and it was brilliant. I was proper glam, just like all the other girls and I had my new boobs to complete the look. This time, the only problem was that my purse was a lot lighter!

I missed Mr Starship while I was there, as it was the first

time I'd been away since first meeting him. I hadn't told him I was going – I thought I would just go and give him a taste of his own medicine. After all, he had disappeared for five days and gone away without telling me, so I decided to do the same back to him.

He called me and I didn't pick up but he obviously realised it was a foreign ring tone and, the next thing, I got a text saying: 'Where are you?'

Well, I wasn't going to tell him so I just texted back: 'Call me *manana*.' I thought using a Spanish word would give him a clue that I was in Spain but he still wouldn't know for sure and that would drive him mad!

When he found out where I was, he went ballistic and stopped speaking to me. I soon realised I had made a mistake and those games weren't going to work with him.

Although I was worrying about Mr Starship, and missed him like mad, me and Ellie had a wicked time. We didn't argue once and became a great double act. We spent our days by the pool and then spent hours getting ready before partying the night away. We didn't see any celebs this time, but we met a lot of nice people, who we partied with.

My time in Marbella was amazing, but I had to come back and face reality: I had no money and I needed to get myself a job – and fast! But I had Mady all week – she was only in nursery for the mornings – so I needed something I could do in the evenings while she was in bed. Ellie worked during the day so she would be at home in the evenings to babysit for me.

Things were rocky between Mr Starship and me, so I didn't want to admit to him that I was skint. I needed a job but I knew that I would have to admit I was broke, so one night I said, 'I really need to get a job and someone has offered me one in a restaurant.'

'No girlfriend of mine is working in a restaurant,' was his response and he told me he would put money into my account, but I never gave him my bank details because I was too embarrassed.

By this point, things were desperate. I needed to make fast money at night when Mady was asleep and there was only one thing I could think of, even though it was something I swore I'd never do. But I needed to support my little girl, and I felt I had no choice.

CHAPTER TEN

Rock Bottom

To this day, none of my family knows what I was doing for money: I was a pole dancer. Sorry, Dad – I know you won't approve, but I need to tell my whole story. You had helped me out enough already; I had to figure out how to survive on my own.

I couldn't bring myself to admit it to anyone apart from Ellie and a couple of other, very close friends. I'm not proud of it but I did what I had to do for my daughter – and I hated absolutely every single minute of it.

Anyway, here's the way it happened.

I felt pole dancing was the only option: I thought it was quick money, and that was what I needed. Plus, I could be there for Mady during the day, bath her, put her to bed and then go to work. I would work until the early hours, drive home, grab a couple of hours' sleep and then get up with Mady. Like a zombie, I would give her breakfast and drop her at nursery, and then collapse back into bed for a few hours.

Now I had never been in one of those clubs before, so I had no idea where to start, but I knew a girl who would. So, I sent her a text asking for some advice. I needed to find out which was the best club in London, somewhere off the beaten track so that I wouldn't risk bumping into anyone I knew. I didn't want anyone to know what I was doing and I was paranoid about people from Essex coming in and recognising me.

She told me about a new club that had just opened in London. The clientele would be mainly City workers so there would be less danger of being recognised. Hardly able to believe it had come to this, I looked up the phone number and rang them. They told me to come in the following day for an audition. Ellie took the afternoon off work so she could have Mady, and I got myself all dressed up and ready. I had no idea what I was supposed to wear, so I put on a classic smart black dress and heels. I did my make-up and false eyelashes as usual and put my hair up in a chignon.

As I drove into London in my clapped-out Toyota Corolla, the whole way I was thinking, 'What am I doing? How did it come to this?' One thing that kept coming into my head was: 'This is not my life.' I had never in a million years dreamed I would be going to audition as a pole dancer.

When I arrived, the manager came to meet me, showed me into the office and asked me to fill in some forms. She then took me into the main club, which was empty because it was the middle of the afternoon, and the first thing that hit me was the smell: it didn't smell nice at all. It was horrible. I kept thinking, 'I can't do this!' but I knew I had no choice because I needed the money to support my daughter and me, and to pay the mounting bills.

The manager sat down at one of the tables right by the stage and said, 'Right, if you want to show me what you can do...'

'Er, what? Sorry, I don't know what you mean,' I stammered.

I didn't realise she would expect me to pole dance! I hadn't thought it through because I didn't want to think about it and I had no dance experience.

I told her I hadn't done it before and I didn't know what to do. Some of the girls who were waiting to start work a bit later had come down to watch my audition and I could feel them whispering and laughing at me. I went bright red and I thought I was going to cry.

The manager then called one of them over and told her to get up on the stage and do a pole dance to show me how it's done.

Well, I just wanted to run out of there and never come back.

This girl smirked at me and obviously decided to put on the show of her life just to show me up, so she really went for it.

She was swinging herself round the pole and flicking her hair all over the place. She was really good.

Now it was my turn to get up there. I was shaking and by this point all the dancers had gathered to watch and probably take the piss, but I knew I had to go through with it. I started trying to dance but I realised that I was wearing totally the wrong outfit. Every time I touched the metal pole, my hand slipped as I was sweating so much – it was like my hands had been dunked in buckets of water. Also, I suffer from slight OCD and all I could think about was how many germs there would be on that pole from all the other girls. I felt sick to the stomach. I looked smart, like I was going to work in an office! Plus, I had my hair up so I couldn't flick it and my shoes weren't right either.

So there I was, with everyone staring at me and for some reason all the nervousness and tension made me start laughing. The whole thing was ridiculous and it goes on the list of one of the scariest things I have ever had to do in my life. I was standing there, auditioning to be a pole dancer and I couldn't even dance!

Once I'd started, I couldn't stop and, eventually, with me in hysterics, the manager told me to get down off the stage. Well, obviously, I thought there wasn't a chance in hell I'd got the job, but the next thing she said was: 'Right, you can start tomorrow night.'

'Er, sorry, *what* did you say?'

'You've got the job, you can start tomorrow night.'

'But I can't dance.'

'Well, you can learn from the other girls.'

I couldn't believe it! Although I'd hated every second of being there that day, I needed the job to solve my problems.

So that was it – I started working at the club and, even though I did get better than I was at that first audition, I really wasn't very good at it and I didn't make much money but anything helped to make ends meet.

Every night, driving over there, all I could think about was how much I hated it and how I wished I could just turn round and go home. But I couldn't. On the way home, I used to cry every night. I would cry because I'd gone from one extreme to another: I had met the man of my dreams and I thought I was going to be a model but, the next thing I know, I'm a dancer with no money, a clapped-out car and no Mr Starship.

Ellie would look after Mady for me so I always knew she was safe. She was really good to me. I often wonder whether, if I hadn't moved Ellie in so soon after me and Mr Starship got together, things might have worked out differently. He started staying over less once she had moved in and, maybe if she hadn't been there, he would have been around more. But I needed her rent and that was that. But I didn't tell Mr Starship – I wouldn't tell him that I couldn't survive without her contribution.

Only a handful of my closest friends knew that I was dancing. I told everyone else that I was a waitress in a top London club. I wished I *was* a waitress but everyone wanted those jobs and there were never any vacancies.

I lasted four months there, the whole time thinking it was just a stopgap until my modelling career took off. Every night, I drove there in my battered old car wondering how my life had gone so wrong.

Things between Mr Starship and me went from bad to worse; I was terrified of him finding out I was working there. As my life became more stressful, his grew busier and we started seeing less of each other. But I needed a night job so I could look after Mady during the day: I wanted to be a good mum to her, and I needed money.

I desperately wanted to get things with Mr Starship back on track. It was nearly his birthday and I was so upset we had not properly made up. Eventually, he got in touch with me by turning up at my house completely out of the blue. He picked me up and drove me to the Prince Regent Hotel in Chigwell. We spoke for hours and he told me he loved me and didn't want to lose me. He even asked me to move to London with him and I agreed. I was so relieved and content. Eventually we went back to mine. I felt terrible because it was nearly his birthday and I hadn't even got him a card. He stayed the night and I woke up early to go out and get him the biggest card I could find! I got him a big card with the words 'To the one I love' on the front. Inside I wrote an essay explaining my feelings. I have always been better at writing my feelings down than saying them. I also wrote that I wanted to take him out for his birthday. I had already planned in my head that I would take him out on a date! I wanted it to be perfect.

I decided to do something extra-special for his birthday at the end of September, even though it wouldn't be on his actual birthday. I bought him a blue Hermès belt and booked us a table at Gordon Ramsay's restaurant Maze in the West End. Mr Starship had never let me pay for dinner before, as he was old-fashioned like that, and I was determined that I was going to buy him a meal for his birthday. I had a plan my dad always used: he would pretend he was going to the toilet and pay the bill discreetly, saving any awkwardness. So, I had decided to do the same to Mr Starship because there was no other way he would let me pay.

As things had turned sour between us, I realised just how much I cared for him and I was determined to put things right. I really loved him and was ready to give him my heart and my life. I went to Lakeside so I could find something classy to wear. I spent ages and finally chose a perfect outfit. Ellie had offered to have Mady for me – she was excited for me! We had decided she would stay on at the cottage when I moved out. I'd still pay half the rent and be able to keep my stuff there, plus I needed a backup in case things didn't work out when I went to live with Mr Starship. Soon the night had arrived and I literally tried on every outfit I owned, which resulted in me being late. I always do that – buy something new and change my mind at the last minute! Stressed and very late I left! I jumped into my car and headed to London.

I remember feeling nervous. I was always conscious of how I looked around him – he was so classy and smart, and I always felt insecure – but I tried not to show my insecurities. I was an hour late, but Mr Starship never complained. He was so laid back. As I walked towards the bar, I had butterflies in my tummy and there he was, handsome and smiling as ever.

The night started off really well; he enjoyed the food and I was floating with happiness. Everything was perfect again. Yes I had hardly any money, and my job was far from what I had dreamed of, but I felt like things would get better now I had the love of my life back. Then he asked what I'd been up to and how my job was going. Dread came over me. I wanted to tell him so badly because I didn't keep secrets from him, but I couldn't. After the meal, we were going to head into the West End to go clubbing. That was the plan, but somewhere along the line it all went pear-shaped and turned into a disaster.

I'd had quite a bit to drink and, when the restaurant closed, I told Mr Starship I was going to the toilet. On the way I paid the bill without him seeing. When I got into the toilet, I realised I looked a bit of a state because I was drunk, so I spent a while re-touching my make-up and that. As I was a bit tipsy, I didn't realise how long I'd been away.

When I came out, Mr Starship had a face like thunder. He thought I'd been making myself sick, but I hadn't. We started having an argument and I just got really upset. Everything had been getting on top of me and it just all came to a head. I was really drained. I was exhausted from working late nights and surviving on just a few hours' sleep because I had to be around for Mady in the morning. I wasn't eating properly and I was making myself sick, so I was weak anyway and just had nothing left. But I wasn't well – I was in the grips of an eating disorder.

All these ups and downs with Mr Starship were making things worse; his antics were making me more miserable. More than anything, I wanted us to be together properly – I felt safe, content and happy when we were together. But then he'd go AWOL and I'd be left devastated. When we were together, it was like being in a bubble where nothing else mattered but, when he wasn't there, I was falling apart. Nothing was going to plan: my modelling career hadn't gone anywhere and as a last resort I was pole dancing, and even that wasn't making me much money.

We went to a nearby bar and carried on drinking – I just wanted to forget everything – and then I suggested going to Chinawhite. By this point, I was really drunk and, when we got there, the club was closed. Like a nutcase, I went mental, screaming at them to let me in – I wasn't having it that they were shut.

In the end, Mr Starship marched me to his car and drove me home. The argument continued the whole way back to Essex. I knew I was making things worse but, in a desperate state, I carried on saying spiteful things. Really, I wanted to cry and say I was sorry. I was desperate to get things back to the way they were but I didn't know how.

It was about 4am by the time we got back to my house and he just chucked me out of the car and drove off, taking my bag, coat, keys, everything with him. It was freezing cold and I lived in the middle of nowhere. Sobbing and shivering, I decided I needed to break in. I took off my wedge shoe and smashed the window with it. Luckily, it was the weekend and Mady was at her grandparents' house and Ellie was staying at a friend's. As I climbed in, I cut my shoulder on the broken glass. I stumbled upstairs and, when I saw all the clothes on the bed that I had laid out earlier as I decided what to wear, I was overcome with emotion. Just a few hours earlier, I had been so happy and excited with the anticipation of the evening ahead.

I broke down. I was screaming, hysterical – how had it all gone so wrong. I knew it was really over now. Then I saw his car pull up and felt a glimmer of hope. I ran down to open the door. He came in and stormed past me; he threw all of my belongings on the couch. By this point, I knew it was over.

I couldn't bear him leaving me on my own, so I ran into the kitchen and grabbed a knife. I stood there with it held to my wrist and screamed, 'I'll do it!' I was standing there, pleading with him not to go. I was crying and saying, 'You are the love of my life.' He was my world. In those few seconds, Mady's face flashed into my mind and I dropped the knife. It hit me what I was thinking about doing and all I could think about was my daughter. I couldn't put my family through any more heartache after what had happened to Tina many years before. In my moment of desperation even though I thought my life was over, I still had enough strength inside to know that I was a mother and I needed to be there for Mady.

Even though I was crying and begging him not to leave, Mr Starship just turned away, got in his car and drove off.

I don't think I've ever felt so upset and alone. I was left sitting on the floor sobbing and I must have stayed like that until the next day when Ellie came home and found me in a right state. 'I don't want to be alive,' I told her – I just couldn't see how anything would get better. I didn't know what to do.

I didn't want to live without him, but I had my beautiful little girl who needed me. I couldn't leave Mady – no one would love her as much as I do. I would be leaving her just as my mum did with me, and I couldn't do that. I couldn't leave her, so I was left dealing with the overwhelming feelings of darkness, sadness and loss. Every day was a struggle.

After that disastrous birthday night, I didn't see Mr Starship for a month. I can honestly say I cried every single day. Every day, I prayed he would get in touch. Even the smallest things were a struggle. I don't know what I would have done without my friend Ellie. She spent hours talking and listening to me and she really helped out with Mady. She was so strong and loyal to me when she could have just walked away.

Ellie then introduced me to a make-up artist called Krystal Dawn Flemming. Krystal was doing a lot of make-up jobs for an agency called Unleashed PR. They also owned a picture agency much like Popstars, with whom I'd already done a shoot. Krystal put me in contact with them, and I went in for a shoot with Harry, the photographer who worked with the agency. On the day of the shoot, I had another glimmer of hope that I could get into glamour modelling. I met both owners of the agency, Craig Johnson-Pass and Emma Hadley. We got on well and the pictures were nice, but unfortunately I was still too skinny, although obviously I didn't know that. And I didn't know those pictures would one day come back to bite me on the bottom, either!

Even though things may have been looking up work-wise, I couldn't think about anything apart from Mr Starship. I lived for Mady and would cry every single day. Every morning, I woke up and realised he wasn't going to be there, I wasn't going to hear his voice or see his face – it was like I was grieving. He completely cut me off. I used to ring his phone and text him long, heartfelt messages but I would get no response.

One day, I noticed his ringtone was a foreign one so I presumed he had taken a holiday. At first, I held out hope that

I would see him the next week. One week turned to a fortnight and I still hadn't heard a single word from him. Everything seemed grey, almost as if I had a horrible raincloud following me around. Nothing made me smile apart from Mady. I seriously felt like my heart was breaking. This was something I had never felt before and I couldn't control it: I was depressed and at rock bottom.

My dad rang and in his caring nice tone he asked me how I was. I burst out crying and he kept asking what was wrong. I never like the thought of burdening my dad as I don't want him worrying about me, but I didn't have anyone else to turn to. I just said, 'Dad, I need help.' I explained about Mr Starship and me breaking up, and he got in his car and drove straight over. He sat with me for a good two hours and he was obviously worried sick. Over the years, my dad has always been there for me when I've needed him and this was no exception. He knew a top private therapist called Bruce in the Oval in London and said he would pay for it. It's usually hard to get an appointment but he was a friend of my dad's and I think he knew I needed help – and fast.

After everything that had happened during my childhood, I kept wondering when I would ever find happiness. The only time I was happy was when I was with Mr Starship. He knew everything, he made me feel safe and loved, and he was really good with Mady. But, when he wasn't around, everything was shit. And most of all I hated my job.

The therapist was totally different to what I expected. He would shout at me to get me to admit how I really felt. I told him all about Mr Starship and he kept saying, 'Who does he remind you of?' I kept saying I didn't know what he meant, but he kept shouting it at me. Eventually, I just shouted back, 'He reminds me of my dad!' I hadn't realised it was true until I said it out loud – I don't think I wanted to admit it to myself but actually they are really alike, both funny but old-fashioned and traditional.

The therapist helped me get stronger by giving me other ways to look at things. He explained to me that I was in a bubble with Mr Starship, and I couldn't see past this bubble, and when we were together inside this bubble I was happy and content. But he would leave the bubble and I'd be left alone, still living in our bubble. It was so true. Although he helped me get stronger, I was never in any doubt that Mr Starship was the love of my life. I continued to have therapy every week for a few months.

Then, a month later, I was in Manchester with Ellie. She and I had planned a big night out as I had never been to Manchester and that's where she is from. We decided Ellie would stay with her granddad and I would stay with our other friend, Jaime (who is also from Manchester), at her mum and dad's. We were really excited and planned our outfits meticulously. Jaime's family were so accommodating and they had a lovely family home. It was the first time in a while that I felt a lot of warmth around me – they were so nice. I was also really excited to go out in Manchester as Ellie had told me what a great night out it was.

There I was, feeling really positive and my phone went. It was a text and there it was in black and white, his name: it was Mr Starship. I didn't know whether to laugh or cry. I had spent a month waiting for this moment and it couldn't have come at a worse time. The text said, 'Are you in Manchester?' and I replied, 'Yes.' He said he wanted to see me but I explained that Ellie and Jaime had gone to a lot of trouble to plan this night out, as well as her family putting themselves out for me to stay, so I couldn't see him that night. He told me he was going out as well and maybe we would see each other later that night.

Ellie and Jaime had hooked us up to go to an exclusive party at a top nightspot called Panacea. It was a private event and there were a lot of faces from London there. We had such a good time and I was secretly buzzing as all the while I was thinking in the back of my mind: 'Is this it? Is the nightmare over? Has he come back for me?'

I didn't end up seeing Mr Starship that night, even though we exchanged a few drunken texts and calls. I didn't see the urgency as surely he had come back to me and changed his mind. We had a great night and I went back to Jaime's with a huge grin on my face, thinking I had my Mr Starship back.

The next day after breakfast, he called. Hearing his voice, now I was sober, felt so familiar, but I still felt as nervous as when I first met him. He made plans to meet me at Living Room in Manchester to talk. Obviously, I had a disgusting hangover and panicked to make sure I looked my best. It was one massive hair and make-up rush. Ellie picked me up and drove me to central Manchester; the whole way there, I was full of nerves and anticipation at seeing him again. I called him when I arrived, but he said he was tied up with something else and couldn't make it. I was so upset. The familiar feeling of disappointment came over me and I started to cry. A wave of depression hit me again. Was I back to square one?

Ellie and I drove back to Jaime's house and they all comforted me. I didn't feel like going anywhere that night but Jaime's family were going to the local working men's club, where her mum worked, and they dragged me down there. I didn't even bother to get changed and, after hours of crying, I certainly wasn't looking my best. When we got there, I cheered up a bit, but just as I started to relax my phone rang. It was him. I considered not answering it, but quickly gave in. As soon as I heard his voice, I knew I would see him that night.

He said he was in a club in Manchester and he wanted me to get a taxi and go and meet him straight away. But I wasn't giving him an easy time on the phone as he had let me down during the day and pretty much ruined my girly weekend. I put the phone down and explained to the girls I needed a taxi. Jaime refused to get me one as we were really far out and argued I didn't know my way around Manchester. I pleaded with her and said, if she didn't help me, I would get one myself. So she got a card and wrote her address, home number and all their mobile phone numbers on it in case I got lost.

Off I went in a minicab, half-excited and half-petrified about where I would end up. I arrived at the club and called Mr Starship. He told me to stand outside and he would come and get me. I was standing there for a good five minutes in my daytime outfit, which consisted of leggings, a pair of cowboy boots and a loose top. It was not my ideal 'seeing Mr Starship' outfit, but what could I do? As I watched people spill out of the club, he appeared.

He looked more handsome than ever, with his familiar smell, voice and laugh. I felt safe again, happy and content that my Mr Starship was once more standing next to me. However, the not knowing, fear and panic of him leaving again overpowered me and, before I knew it, I was going mad and shouting at him.

We stayed together that night and the next morning the argument wasn't mentioned, but I didn't know if it had been forgotten. After we had breakfast together, he gave me a lift back to Jaime's house in a taxi. As I got out of the cab, so did he. We stood and spoke, then cuddled, and he said he would pick me up later that day. We said goodbye, and off he went. I watched his taxi until I couldn't see it any more. I could feel the tears welling up and, as the taxi turned the corner, I broke down crying. Would he really come back? Even though I'd been up all night, I got ready and waited for him. He never came back. I called him and he was cold and distant, completely different to how he'd been earlier that day. He said he was with his mum. Earlier that day, he had said he would introduce me to his mum for the first time, but it wasn't mentioned again. I told him I was leaving to go back to Essex in a few hours and he said he would try to see me before I left.

I waited for as long as I could but I had to get back for Mady, who had stayed at her grandparents'. So, me and Ellie packed the car up and started the long drive back to Essex. I cried all the way home, which was a good four hours. I could still hear his voice and smell him on me, but I felt life was over. Ellie was trying to console me, bless her, but it wasn't working – nothing she could say would take away this pain. He called me later that day, told me he missed me. It sounded like he was at an airport – his voice was quiet, almost sad. It was awful. I didn't move from my bed for two days. Ellie was my rock once again; she took care of me. Eventually, I had to pull myself together for Mady.

As it turned out, I didn't see him again for a year and seven months but I didn't know that then. Throughout the whole time, he kept making promises that he would come but he never did. I never stopped hoping maybe the next day would be the day he'd be back and he'd walk through the door.

It was the lowest point of my whole life: I had no money, I was completely skint and I'd lost the love of my life. I was fucked. I couldn't pay the rent or the bills. My landlord was threatening to kick us out and we had nowhere to go.

I couldn't pay the gas bill so it got cut off. Nearly winter, it was getting colder. We had no hot water so I would boil a kettle to bath Mady. I would put a washing-up bowl in the middle of the lounge floor in front of an electric heater and fill up the bowl from the kettle and bath her like that. Then I'd put two pairs of pyjamas on her to keep her warm at night.

My plans to be a good mum had failed: I had hit rock bottom. But I had to pick myself up and sort myself out. My house was like a squat – everything was falling apart – and I desperately needed to move out of there. I worked out that I needed £2,000 to move out. That would be enough to pay for a deposit and the first couple of months' rent on a new place. So, although I hated every minute of it, I went back to pole dancing.

The club was getting busier as it became more established and I started making good money. I was tired all the time but I just had to get through each week and then, at the weekends, I could sleep all day.

I found a house and I was determined to make enough money to move there. It was a lovely little three-bedroom cottage in Chigwell and, most importantly, it was warm and cosy with plenty of room for me, Mady and Ellie. I had got myself into arrears with the rent and the bills and I needed to make a fresh start.

As soon as I had saved the £2,000 I needed, I went straight to pay the deposit and the rent up front. Then I had literally one day to get out of my old place so I packed up the most important things and did a moonlight flit. I had to run away from the house and I left no forwarding address or anything. I didn't pay the rent I owed and I felt terrible about it, but it was either pay them the money or get Mady a safe, warm new home. I had to put my daughter first and I did feel bad, but the whole place was falling apart. The landlord didn't deserve that, though, and I have felt guilty about it ever since. But back then I just needed to make a fresh start and that was the only way.

I couldn't fit everything in my car and couldn't risk going back so I left loads of things behind. I still feel gutted about some of Mady's baby things that I left. Her little hospital bracelet that she had worn the day she was born was one of the things that got left behind – it still upsets me because I wanted to treasure that forever.

I had to start again – and I was determined not to look back. It was coming up to Christmas again and I needed to make money to buy presents. I was still adamant that pole dancing was only a stopgap and I thought, if I could just get through Christmas, then I could leave.

Every night after I left the club, I cried. All the way home to Essex, I would be sobbing – I missed Mr Starship and hated how my life had turned out. I was really sad and I wondered why my life had turned out so shit. I was still making myself sick and I wasn't getting any better.

Even though I already thought I'd hit rock bottom, things got even worse before they got better. Matthew had gone AWOL, so Mady was spending every weekend with his mum and dad. I was getting really annoyed with him for letting her down. I wanted to make her Christmas as special as the one before and make sure she had just as many presents, especially as she was getting a bit older and understanding it more.

December was a busy time at the club. I was working every single night because it was such a good chance to make some cash but I was absolutely burnt out.

One morning, I woke up feeling terrible – I was shivering and shaking, and realised I had caught flu. I lay in bed crying because I felt so sick with flu and all I wanted to do was stay in bed, but it was going to be the busiest night yet at the club and I couldn't afford not to go to work. So I dragged myself out of bed and forced myself to get dressed. I was still feeling ill and it was freezing, so I put on a long sheepskin coat over my dress and got into my car. I set off and after only a few minutes I realised there was something wrong with my car – it was making a terrible noise but I kept on driving anyway because I needed to get to work. I made it to the Hackney Road when finally it just broke down. I could see steam coming from the bonnet and I just stood there in the middle of the road, crying. I was ill and cold, and I just couldn't see a way out – I actually wanted someone to run me over so it would all go away.

I rang a male friend – Cem – and was crying so much he could barely understand what I was saying. A few months earlier, I'd met him in a London club when he'd chatted me up. We'd got talking and he seemed nice, so I gave him my number and agreed to go on a date. We went out once but all I could think about was Mr Starship so it was never going to go anywhere, but we did get on so ended up keeping in touch as friends. He proved what a good friend he was to me that day. I told him I had broken down on the Hackney Road, there was steam coming out of my car and I didn't know what to do. I was hysterical.

Cem lived in Hertfordshire – about an hour from where I was – but he told me he would come and get me. He got a cab all the way to meet me and, when I saw him, I started crying even more because I was overwhelmed by his kindness. He had a look under the bonnet and said it seemed like the radiator. After he poured some water in, the engine started. He began driving towards my work but it kept overheating so he kept pulling over and pouring more water in. Eventually, we made it to work, stopping and starting the whole way. I sat in my car and just sobbed because I was so poorly and miserable. When I looked in the car mirror, I looked horrendous – I had mascara all down my face!

There was no way I could go to work – I couldn't stop crying and I looked a total wreck. Cem could see what a mess I was in and he just said, 'There is no way you are going to work. You are really ill – you need to go to bed.'

I told him I needed the money and I didn't have any choice. He said no and gave me some money out of his own pocket. He said I could pay him back when I had money.

I was so grateful I started crying even more. Once I'd got myself together, he helped me fill the car up with water again and I set off on the long drive back to Essex – stopping and starting all the way to pour more water in. I was so relieved when I got home – I had never been so glad to get in my bed in all my life! I have never forgotten what Cem did for me that day, and we are still friends now. We don't see each other that often because we are both so busy, but we still speak on the phone.

The next morning, I felt a bit better and I needed to sort my car out. I couldn't go to work with no car. I didn't know what to do, so I rang my dad and told him what had happened. He got a mechanic friend of his to come and take a look at it and he told me it was fucked. So, I phoned my dad again and was really upset. He was brilliant – he said I could borrow his car for a couple of weeks and he would share Karen's because they were both off work over Christmas and New Year.

So, for the next week, I worked all the hours I could and had enough money to buy all my Christmas presents and the tree, with some left over. And I had my dad's car until the New Year, when he would need it back.

I got all the presents and, again, planned a lovely day for Mady and me in our new house, but I was still devastated over Mr Starship. I was crying every day and was so miserable – even my new home didn't feel right without him.

When it got to New Year, the first thing I needed to do was get myself a new car. I had enough for a deposit but there was no way I could get a car loan because I had a poor credit rating and no one would have given me the finance. I told my friend all about the mess I was in and they told me they would get a car on finance for me in their name. I was so grateful – my friend has been really good to me over the years and I was overwhelmed by this kindness.

We went to the garage and I chose a Golf – it was perfect. It was only a couple of years old and it was all mine. I loved that car.

I had a nice house and a nice car now, but I was still so miserable. I was heartbroken. Every day was grey and I felt like I had a big black cloud hanging permanently over my head. I felt so low – it all just seemed so shit and pointless. I knew I was depressed and that I must do something about it for Mady's sake as much as my own: she deserved to have a happy mum. I needed to help myself and sort my head out.

No one held out any hope that I would eventually be with Mr Starship properly apart from Ellie. She has been such an amazing friend to me. I cried with her so many times, and at times she even cried too, because she could see how much I was hurting. She would sit with me for hours on end, comforting me.

I knew no one else would ever come close to Mr Starship –

it was proper true love – and so I decided I had to get him back somehow.

I started feeling a bit better in myself and I hadn't been making myself sick so often, but I had no energy and I needed this to be able to work and make money. It was also becoming harder and harder to make myself sick – it was as if my body wouldn't physically let me be sick. I had started to feel unwell and my throat had become really sore from all the puking.

Plus, Mr Starship knew all about my eating disorder and I thought maybe that was partly why he didn't want me. I kept thinking, 'Who could blame him? Why on earth would he want to be with someone who was weak, skint and had an eating disorder to boot?' So I made a vow to try to get stronger, to be the woman he deserved.

Then there was my glamour-modelling career. It had been nearly a year since my first photoshoot and nothing had come of it. I had to face the fact that modelling hadn't worked out for me, but I hated working as a pole dancer, so I knew something needed to change.

The previous summer in Marbella, some of the girls I had met over there had been talking about the Playboy mansion in LA. They told me all about the Playboy girls out there, and at the time I thought it sounded amazing. It seemed there was more money in glamour modelling over in the States and I really wanted to go over there. My best friend Ellie was still working for Simon Webbe and she had told me that he had loads of contacts out in LA, and he would be able to introduce me to some people who could help me.

So, I spoke to Simon and he told me the dates when he was going to be over in LA and said, if I could sort out a flight, we could meet up and he'd take me to meet some influential people out there. This was my big chance so I checked out the prices of flights and worked out how much I needed to save.

Although I hated the pole dancing, the thought of LA kept me going.

Even though I was trying my hardest to forget about Mr Starship, I still missed him so much it hurt. My friends told me I couldn't pine forever and that I had to move on, so I went on a few dates. I would agree to go out with someone and would be determined to give them a chance, but they always ended the same – I'd have a drink to calm my nerves and then look at them and think, 'You're not Mr Starship.' I'd end up telling them, 'I'm still in love with my ex,' and sometimes I'd even start crying, so it wasn't surprising none of them ever worked out. I knew it was pointless, those guys couldn't compare to him. Ever.

I felt so frustrated. He had abandoned me so he didn't deserve my love or my loyalty, but I just couldn't move on. Day-to-day life was hard because there was always something that reminded me of him – songs, places and memories. Something would trigger a memory and I'd just break down in tears.

Ellie convinced me to pick myself up a little, get my glad rags on and have a well-deserved night out. There was a private party in London that one of Ellie's friends was organising, at a club called 50. So, Ellie, Helen, Jaime and me got dressed up and made our way there.

We were in the VIP area when a guy came up and started talking to me. Good-looking and funny, he asked if he could buy me a drink. We chatted, but, every time I went to go to the bar, he would block the way and ask, 'Where are you going?' When I explained that I was going to the bar, he gestured for the waitress who supplied us with drinks; he didn't let me buy a drink all night. He wasn't English – he was from Europe – and had just moved to a famous part of Manchester. He told me he had just split up with his girlfriend back home and seemed like a genuine nice guy. Although he was a couple of years younger than me, he seemed mature.

He asked me for my number, so I gave it to him – he seemed nice and I liked him – and, even though he wasn't Mr Starship, I was trying to move on because I knew I had to at some point.

We went on a few dates and eventually I slept with him. The first time we slept together, I cried afterwards because Mr Starship wasn't the last person I'd slept with any more. It went from there and we were seeing each other for a couple of months. Every few weeks, he would fly me up to Manchester. Although I was still in love with Mr Starship, I liked him more and more and thought he felt the same.

One weekend, I went up as usual and, when we met this time, I had the shock of my life: he was wearing a wedding ring. It turned out he had been married all along and he had been taking his ring off every time I saw him. This time he had forgotten.

I was really upset that he had lied to me and that he was just another lying arsehole. I have decided not to name him – not because I give a shit about him – but because he has a wife and kids and I feel it's not fair on them. They didn't cheat and they don't deserve it.

Although I was upset about it, I was also angry and I decided that was that – I was swearing off men for a while. They all just turned out to be liars anyway. I focused on my trip to LA and tried to think of the positives. Unfortunately, when it came to it, I just didn't have enough money for the flight and the dates weren't going to work out, so I had to scrap that idea.

The worst bit about my life was my job. I desperately needed to get out of being a pole dancer. I hated everything about it. I was getting stronger and I realised that it was dragging me down. I came to the decision that I would rather have no money than work there – and then out of the blue came a fantastic opportunity.

I really believe that, if you want something badly enough, something will happen to make it a reality and that's exactly what happened.

I was on a night out at Cirque Du Soir in the West End – which is a club that has circus performers in it – when one of the waitresses came up to me. She was French, and she asked if I was a model. I told her I wasn't, but I had always wanted to be and we got chatting. She told me she worked for Playboy and that they were looking for a bunny to work in France. It was like a dream come true. I had been dying to go to the Playboy mansion and now here was someone offering me work for Playboy!

It seemed too good to be true; I had been offered so many things in the past that for one reason or another hadn't materialised. Although I tried not to get my hopes up, it was impossible not to because it was such a great opportunity. I was determined to seize it with both hands and not let it slip away, like all the others.

I'd been at rock bottom and I knew I didn't ever want to go back there again. I thought this could be my big break.

The waitress gave me a card with an email address on it and told me to email some pictures over to the French Playboy bosses. So, I went home all excited and got straight on the computer and sent over some photos.

I got an email back saying they wanted me to go to Paris. I couldn't believe it! They wanted to book me and asked me to go to Paris to meet them in February 2010. They booked me on the Eurostar and arranged a hotel. I was so excited; it felt like a dream.

When I arrived, I checked into the hotel and the bosses – two French guys called Nicholas and Guillaume – came and met me and took me out for dinner. We went to a really posh place called La Cantine for sushi. It all felt surreal.

The bosses were really nice and explained that I would get paid €250 for every personal appearance. My job would be to promote the Playboy brand. I couldn't believe my luck! Basically, they toured around France, going to casinos and prestigious nightclubs to promote Playboy. All I had to do was wear the official Playboy bunny outfit, which they had specially made for me. It was a brilliant opportunity and, of course, I said yes straight away. Because the job was only at weekends, Mady would be at her grandparents' anyway, so I wouldn't need to change any of her routine.

I went back to the UK and quit pole dancing – I just never

went back. I felt a huge weight lift off my shoulders, knowing I never had to go back there again.

Now I knew I would be earning better money I decided that Mady and me needed to live on our own, so I asked Ellie to move out. Mady had started school by then, and I decided it wasn't right to have my friend living with us – we needed to be a proper family, just the two of us. Plus, now I wouldn't be working nights any more, I wouldn't need Ellie to babysit as she had before. She was great about it and got herself a flat not too far away and we still saw each other all the time.

I rented a flat for me and Mady in Buckhurst Hill, above the shops on Queens Road. By pure coincidence, it was just a few doors down from the flat where Matthew had first moved in with me, all those years before. It wasn't ideal because it was noisy, but it was our little home, away from the rest of the world.

Mady was growing into such an amazing little girl and we have always been really close because it's just the two of us. She still sleeps in my bed now she's seven and we are inseparable. She's a really happy, confident little girl and always asks millions of questions. She is also a little show-off, always singing and dancing.

So, with my pole-dancing days behind me, I started my new life working in France that weekend.

CHAPTER ELEVEN

Turning a Corner

The best thing about the Playboy job was that I could work weekends when Mady was with her grandparents, meaning I could be at home all week, which was exactly what I wanted. I wanted to be there to give her breakfast and take her to school. And I wanted to be there to pick her up from school, give her tea and put her to bed. I didn't want to be away.

So the job was perfect – I could take her to school on a Friday morning, go straight to Stansted and fly to whichever city in France we were going to. All my flights and travel were paid for. I would do two PAs on Friday and Saturday nights, which would make me €500, and then fly home on the Sunday.

The PAs involved wearing my Playboy bunny outfit,

mingling in the clubs and then posing for photos with the clubbers. At the end of the night, we would stand on stage and throw free stuff, like Playboy key rings, into the crowd. I was always introduced as an official Playboy bunny from London and the French people treated me like I was famous!

On my first day, the bosses had told me that I would meet up with the other Playboy bunny at Stansted and we would fly over together. Her name was Ann French and she was originally from Newcastle but lived in Luton. We hit it off immediately.

Ann was really lovely and well spoken, and came from a nice well-to-do family but, despite our different backgrounds, we became good friends. She was really pretty – she looked like the movie star Megan Fox. We had a lot in common because we were both trying to make a living from modelling.

My life soon fell into a regular pattern. I was going to France every weekend and earning decent money. Things were looking up, but Mr Starship was on my mind all the time – I still felt that he was The One – and I wanted to show him that I had made a success of my life.

It was around this time in early 2010 that I first heard about the new reality TV show based in Essex that was being planned and I had my first meeting with the producer.

By this time, I was being offered even more work with Playboy. That May, I went to Cannes for the Film Festival, which was absolutely amazing. Dressed as a white bunny, I went to all the best parties. I was rubbing shoulders with proper A-listers. One night, I was in a club and Paris Hilton and her sister Nicky were standing right next to me! After

Cannes, we went on to St Tropez, which was unlike anything I had ever seen before – there was just so much glamour around.

Working for Playboy made me even more conscious of the way I looked. I was hanging around with glamour models and I got sucked into their way of thinking that everything should be exaggerated, from your boobs to your lips. One of the girls I met was shocked when I told her I'd never had Botox before. She couldn't believe it; they were all doing it. I had never even thought about it but once I realised how good it was, I was hooked. I've been having it ever since.

I also decided to get my lips done. I'd had fillers around my mouth a couple of years earlier, but nothing more. Mr Starship would never have let me have anything like that done. He likes classy-looking girls. He hates the plastic look, which is quite ironic!

I had collagen in my lips and they were ridiculous, so I've never had that done again. Now I stick to Botox and fillers. At the time, I didn't realise they were so big because everyone around me looked the same – I forgot about the real world. Looking back now, with my dyed-blonde hair, I looked like a Swedish porn star!

Throughout all this, I was becoming really close to Ann as we spent a lot of time together. She was dating Nicholas, one of the bosses, and I found myself attracted to the other boss, Guillaume. He was French and always seemed a bit mysterious. He didn't really speak much English so I hadn't got to know him that well and I found that I wanted to. One night after we'd been at a club doing a PA, we went back to the hotel, had a few drinks and I kissed him.

He was ten years older than me – I was 28 and he was 38 – and was a genuinely nice guy. I was feeling lonely and he comforted me, always there for a cuddle when I needed one. I hadn't had any physical contact with a man for months, and we started seeing each other and eventually we slept together.

Although I didn't feel the same way about Guillaume as I had about Mr Starship, I carried on seeing him for a good eight months because he was nice and treated me like a princess. I really didn't like having sex with him but I only had to see him at weekends. It was clear from the start that I wasn't with him for the right reasons but I was lonely and didn't want to admit it was wrong.

Plus, I had a nice set-up. There was Ann and Nicholas, then Guillaume and me as the perfect foursome. One weekend, we didn't have any PAs booked, so Guillaume said he would come to London and stay with me. He had told me he wanted to go and see a boxing match, so I sorted out tickets through a friend of a friend and we had a nice evening.

When we got back to my flat, he declared his undying love for me. As soon as he said, 'I love you,' I went cold. He asked me to move to France and be with him properly but it just filled me with dread. There was no spark between us, but I still refused to admit it. I had got to know Guillaume and he was lovely, so I was trying to convince myself that I could be with him. I was trying to get over Mr Starship, but at the end of the day he just couldn't compare.

I told myself I could do it, that this could work, but I didn't love Guillaume. And the more intense he became, the more I wanted to get away from him. He wanted to have sex all the

Pre-surgery.

Modelling days.

After ending my relationship with Matthew, I got back into the party scene and hit-up all the best London venues. It was during this time I was to meet the love of my life.

Above left: I love getting dressed up for a night out.

Above right: Chinawhite in 2008.

Below: Here I am posing with Ellie, one of my best friends.

It was also around this time my bulimia started to take hold.

Above: My best friends. From left: Ellie, Frankie, me and Helen.

Below: My extended family. From left: Nanny Linda, Dad, my brother, Dad's wife Karen, Frankie, Joey, my sister Demi, me and my sister Frankie (below).

After missing out on Series One of *TOWIE*, I never thought I'd get the chance to be part of one of the best shows on TV. I've met so many new people.

Above: I love Joey to bits. Here we are with Nanny Linda in 2011 at the Essex Polo.

Below: Celebrating my 30th Birthday in 2011. From left: Madison, Lauren Pope, Frankie, me and Lauren Goodger.

Mady loves the cast, too. Here she is with her favourite member Tom Pearce!

time, but I never enjoyed doing it with him – I just didn't want him on me.

I remember one night we were in a hotel somewhere in France – all the places merged into one after a while – and Guillaume had been pestering me for sex. He'd been on at me before we had gone out, but I'd managed to put him off. Then, when we got home, he was pawing me again and I decided that I would have to go through with it. I was staring out of the window into the blackness of the night and all I could think about was Mr Starship. I felt tears come into my eyes. I couldn't fight it any longer – I was still in love with Mr Starship.

It became a nightmare, with Guillaume always trying it on. It got to the stage where I would do anything to get out of it – not the way a relationship should be at all. I would dread seeing him because I knew that I would have to have sex with him, and I'd make up any excuse not to do it. All I could think about was that I wanted Mr Starship. I had started to allow myself to reminisce and I would lie in bed with Guillaume, thinking about the love of my life. If Guillaume even dared to touch me while I was thinking about Mr Starship, I would feel like smacking him round the face.

At the same time, I was becoming closer and closer to Ann, and one day she tackled me about my bulimia. We were spending long periods of time together, travelling from place to place, eating together and she had noticed the signs.

She was a real straight-talker and just came out with 'I know you are making yourself sick'. I was about to deny it but I was tired and didn't have the energy to lie – plus, I could tell by her face that she was on to me. So, I told her everything, literally poured my heart out to her. And she helped me get over my eating disorder: she made me see I was too skinny. She stood next to me in front of the mirror and made me look at her figure and then look at mine.

I realised then that she was right – she was slim, but not skinny and she had a lovely figure. I was all skin and bone, and it wasn't attractive. At first, it was hard to stop, and having food in my stomach made me feel bloated, but with Ann's help I fought the bulimia. It wasn't an overnight cure, but by taking it one day at a time I managed to overcome it. I will never be able to thank her enough for the way she helped me. She became a really close friend.

I also confessed that I couldn't stand Guillaume – it all just came out – and, once I'd said it out loud, there was no going back. The whole sad story came tumbling out about how I was still so in love with Mr Starship and I couldn't bear being with Guillaume.

If it hadn't been so tragic, it would have been funny. I'd finally landed a wicked job, got together with a really lovely bloke who was my boss and was really into me, but I just didn't feel the same way. And then everything got depressing again. The job I had loved had lost its appeal because I just associated it with Guillaume and having to have sex with him. It had reached the stage where I began to hate him. I would sit on the plane the whole way there, thinking, 'I don't want to go and have sex,' and it was getting me down.

I was also getting fed up of the whole thing. I was sick of flying. Every Friday morning, I had to rush to Stansted, panicking that I would miss my flight and then all weekend I'd either be travelling from place to place, stuck in a packed club or be asleep. I didn't have any free time because I was looking after Mady all week and working all weekend. I needed a break.

The clubs we would go to were always in the middle of nowhere. Sometimes we'd land at an airport and then have to drive for hours and hours to where we were going. The following day, we'd be back in the car, driving for hours again to the next place. It was exhausting. I was fed up of travelling.

By this point, I had missed my chance to be in *TOWIE* and I was gutted. I realised what a massive mistake I'd made that day at the airport. Dreading going to France as usual, I saw Sam Faiers, Lydia Bright and Amy Childs on the front covers of all the magazines.

I just thought it was typical – yet again, I had missed out on a fantastic opportunity. But, when I'd had the initial meetings, things were going well for me and I hadn't known everything was about to turn to shit yet again.

And I was missing Mr Starship so much that one day I just decided I needed to tell him how I felt. There was no point being in love with him and him not knowing – I had to tell him. So, I rang him and he texted back. He seemed pleased to hear from me and we started talking again.

By this time, he was living out in Miami, so he asked me if we could Skype. The first time, I was really nervous about seeing his face again but, as soon as I saw it, I realised I was still so in love with him. I was so grateful to be back in touch with him again – I needed him in my life to make me happy. I was only happy when we were speaking, and, when we weren't in touch, I was miserable.

I have never felt the way I feel about Mr Starship about anyone else before. I've never really enjoyed sex with anyone else – we have a magical connection I've never had with anyone else. He's like a drug – I am hooked on him, and he's all I can think about. I love everything about him – I love his toes, I love his legs, his bum and his stomach.

I love his eyes, his smile, his laugh, his voice.

He is impulsive, kind and funny, and he's got a piss-taking sense of humour which I love. He's a joker and he is always messing around singing and dancing and making me laugh. Even when I'm sad, he can always make me laugh.

And he is confident – he is strong, physically and mentally, and he makes me feel safe. Ever since I was a little girl and my dad took me to Chicago to stay with my granddad, I have been scared of the dark. That image from the night when I saw the shadow and thought there was a man standing there has stayed with me all these years. When Mady and me are on our own, I always make sure everything is locked. I leave a light on, close the door and put a barricade behind it so no one can get in. The only time I'm not afraid of the dark is when I'm with Mr Starship.

He still gives me butterflies to this day: I love him, and I always will.

We started talking again two years ago and I just knew it wasn't over between us. He had never told me it was over – it had always been left wide open. And, even though I hadn't seen him for over a year and a half, I was still as in love with him as I had ever been.

He had set up a business in Miami and was making a life for himself over there. I wanted to prove to him that I was making a success of my own life too. He is always so calm and in control, never aggressive and he never swears. He's a real gentleman.

Even though I was 100 per cent sure I was in love with Mr Starship, I was still going out with Guillaume because I didn't know how I could possibly dump him and still do my job. I had started telling him I was busy and was seeing him less and less, working only the minimum I needed to get by.

It was my 29th birthday at the beginning of November and I decided I would organise something extra special to celebrate. I had made good money working for Playboy and had a bit saved up, so I booked a table at Nobu in Berkeley Square for me and a few of my closest friends – including my best friend Ellie and my old school friend Helen.

I also decided that I needed to change my look – I had started thinking maybe it was the Swedish porn-star look that was making me so unlucky in love. I was attracting the wrong types, like the married man living in Manchester, because I looked fake – I needed to tone my look down. So I dyed my hair really dark brown and had long extensions put in. I was really pleased with it and I wanted to show it off.

As my birthday fell on a weeknight, I would have Mady, so I phoned Matthew a few weeks beforehand to ask if he could babysit. She sees her dad most weekends when she stays with his mum and dad, but I hoped the fact it was a special occasion meant that he would help out and look after our daughter, so I would be able to go out for my birthday. I got all dressed up and ready to go, wearing a really tight white dress. I was feeling happy because I was back in touch with Mr Starship and excited about going out. In the past, Mr Starship had always remembered my birthday – 2 November – and the anniversary of the day we met – 24 November – so I was expecting to hear from him.

But the night got off to a bad start when Matthew didn't turn up at the time we had arranged. I was ringing his phone and he wasn't answering. I was fuming. Yet again a man was about to ruin my night.

In the end, I rang his mum and dad's house to see if they had seen him. His dad Brian answered and said he had no idea where he was. I explained that I was meant to be going out and was all dressed and ready. By this time, Mady was in bed asleep and I was really upset. All my friends were there waiting for me! Brian could tell how disappointed I was. Joan, Matthew's mum, was already out so she couldn't babysit, but Brian said he would do it. Bless him, he got straight in his car and came round, and I was really touched. I will never forget that he did that for me when his son couldn't be bothered to look after his own daughter. Brian sat in the chair all night and waited up for me to come home; it was so kind of him.

The girls and me had a lovely meal in Nobu and then we decided to head to Funky Buddha afterwards, which had always been *the* place to go on a Tuesday night.

When we arrived at the club, there were loads of paparazzi outside because *The Only Way Is Essex* stars Mark Wright,

James 'Arg' Argent and Mark's sister Jess were all in there. Everyone was making a real fuss of them and again I couldn't help thinking what a massive mistake I'd made.

I'd had a few drinks and I wanted to hear my song, 'You Are My Starship' – the one from our very first date – so I went to ask the DJ if he could play it. Anyway, one of the bouncers saw me heading towards the DJ box and came and grabbed me. He told me I was drunk and that I had to leave. I told him I wasn't drunk, it was my birthday and that I was just asking for a song. He was having none of it and marched me up the stairs and tried to throw me out.

I made a fuss and one of the other bouncers came over and asked what was going on. 'Listen, I'm not leaving,' I said, and I just stood at the top of the stairs. They told me that, if I waited there for a bit, they would let me back in. Anyway, the next thing I see is Ellie being dragged up the stairs – they were trying to throw her out as well! She had seen me being marched up the stairs and thought I was being thrown out, so she'd kicked off on my behalf.

They told me I could go back in, but Ellie was barred, so in the end we both left. I was in a mood because I still hadn't heard from Mr Starship so I sent him a text saying 'thanks for remembering my birthday'.

As we walked out, Layla Manoochehri – who was Simon Webbe's girlfriend at the time – said she was leaving as well and was off to another club, Luxx, which was nearby. We had just walked in when my phone rang. It was Mr Starship. I desperately wanted to speak to him, but it was too noisy in the club and so I ran out, but I was wearing ridiculous heels and

I missed a step and landed on my knees! Automatically I kept my phone in the air and the call was still connected. I landed right in front of a bouncer, who looked down at me and automatically lifted me up like I was a puppet. I don't know whether it was the bouncer's kindness, Mr Starship's voice or the pain in my knees, but suddenly I was in floods of tears on my birthday.

So, I ended my night sitting on the pavement crying, with my mascara dripping down my face and bleeding knees, telling Mr Starship that I missed him. And I couldn't help wondering why nothing in my life ever seems to go to plan. These things only ever seem to happen to me!

After that, we were speaking on the phone all the time, and on Christmas Day he rang me and we had a long chat. We wanted to see each other but he was over in Miami and I was still working in France and had Mady to think about, so I couldn't just drop everything. On Boxing Day, I was at home on my own, because Mady was with Matthew and his parents, when my mobile rang. It was a model friend of mine.

I answered her call and yet again something totally unexpected happened. She explained that her and a few friends were going to Miami to celebrate New Year's Eve, and one of the girls had pulled out. My heart sank. She explained there was a spare place at their hotel and the flights were already booked. The girl who had pulled out couldn't get a refund, so the place was mine if I wanted it. All I had to do was pay to change the name on the flight to mine! I didn't have much money, but this felt like fate and I didn't want to miss the opportunity.

As soon as she said Miami, all I could think about was Mr Starship – I hadn't seen him for a year and seven months, and I missed him like mad. And I was being offered a free trip to the same place where he was living!

I must have gone totally speechless because she carried on talking about the trip. I had no idea what to say – it was already Boxing Day and the trip was in four days' time. I told her that I didn't think I could do it – it just seemed too much.

As soon as I put the phone down, I rang Mr Starship and told him about it. He told me I should go and I realised he was right. This was my opportunity to see him again! I couldn't believe I had said no to her offer. So, I rang her straight away and told her I had changed my mind. She was over the moon!

So, four days later, after hurriedly arranging for Mady to stay with Matthew's mum and dad for the four days, off I went. The other girls were travelling separately, as most of them lived up north, so I was going on my own.

I couldn't sleep on the flight over – I was so excited and nervous at the same time. When I landed at the airport, I took a taxi, which took me to where I'd be staying. It was a huge building – one side of it was a hotel and the other was residential. The girls and me would be staying in a flat, which they had hired, on the residential side.

Mr Starship rang me and said he would take me for coffee. He told me to go down in the lift and he would see me in the foyer. I was waiting in reception when he rang me and said, 'Come outside!' He stayed on the phone and said, 'You look nice – I like your outfit.' Spinning around, I was trying to look for him but I couldn't see him. I was saying, 'Where are you?'

and he was just winding me up and saying, 'Your hair looks nice,' and freaking me out. Then a big American truck pulled up. It was dark outside so I couldn't see past his headlights. The car pulled towards me and there he was.

I ran over to meet him, got in the car and he drove us to a coffee house nearby. I'd been so nervous about seeing him but he was just so familiar that all my nerves melted away. He even smelled the same and I realised my feelings for him were as strong as ever. It was so nice to see him in person again but I just started crying. I couldn't help it – I think I was crying for all the hurt I'd been through since the last time I'd seen him.

I could have sat with him in that coffee shop all night, but I had to go back to the apartment to get ready for a night out with the others. That was what I was there for, after all, and I didn't want to let the girls down. When he dropped me back at my hotel, he gave me a phone that he had put credit on and put his number in. It was so sweet of him as he didn't want me to run up a big phone bill when I was out there.

I was running so late for dinner, which was typical Mr Starship. So I said goodbye to him, ran through the lobby of the hotel side and then back out through the exit of the residential side, where a taxi was waiting for me. I was greeted by some very impatient faces, so I apologised and off we went for dinner.

After dinner, we went to a club nearby. Mr Starship and I had been texting throughout the night and he said he would come to the same club. I arrived and there was no sign of him. I couldn't help but look for him. About half an hour later, Mr Starship appeared – just seeing him there took my breath away. I went over to speak to him and he was with a group of friends. I was absolutely gutted – instead of introducing me, he just talked to me as if I was someone he hardly knew.

I'd been so nervous about seeing him and so miserable without him that I just lost it – I threw myself on him and started trying to strangle him. I told him I hated him and that he had ruined my life.

In the end, I went running back to my apartment in tears. Luckily, it was nearly the end of the night, so I knew the girls wouldn't be too annoyed with me for storming off. As I ran through the foyer, with my mascara streaming down my face, the poor concierge didn't know where to look.

The next morning, I felt awful – I couldn't believe I had ruined our reunion, so I rang him to apologise and he seemed fine.

That day was New Year's Eve and one of the girls had organised for us to go to a special fancy-dress party. Now I hate fancy-dress parties – if someone invites me to one I never go, or if I do then I don't dress up. I just don't like them. But, it was New Year's Eve and if the other girls were doing it, then I had to get involved. So, I decided that, if I was going to do it, I might as well take it seriously. I went in 70s flower-power fancy dress – I was wearing a huge Afro wig. Me and the other girls spent ages getting ready and I managed to relax and enjoy myself.

By now, I was getting on really well with everyone on the holiday, especially because I hadn't met all of them before. The club was decorated amazingly, they must have spent thousands. We had the best table – right in the middle of the club. As I ordered my first drink, my little mobile rang. I knew who it was without even looking as he was the only one who had the number.

Mr Starship told me he was spending New Year's Eve somewhere else because he wasn't happy with me. He told me he understood why I was so emotional and said he thought it would be better if we spent the night separately as he didn't want to see me in a drinking environment. He told me to enjoy my night and not to worry. I explained to him about my ridiculous fancy-dress outfit and told him I was disappointed I wouldn't get to wear my special New Year's Eve dress. 'Well, maybe you will get to wear it tomorrow,' he said. I told him that I wasn't going out the next day as it was my last night but he just laughed. 'Aren't you?' he said, and I got that familiar feeling of excitement.

I decided to at least try to enjoy myself and it turned out to be a really good night. I had a few drinks and the girls were all really fun. At midnight, we exchanged texts and I was really happy. Towards the end of the evening, I was told the club were hosting an after party at a mansion. I decided it might be fun, and I was intrigued to see what the mansion might be like. I needed the toilet and one of the club promoters we were with offered to take me there as the club was packed. As he led me through the crowd, my phone rang. It was Mr Starship. I was delighted – I wasn't expecting to hear from him – so I answered his call and he just said, 'Why is that guy holding your wrist?' At first I was so confused but then I realised he was in the club! He was laughing, but all I could say was, 'Are you in here?' He just chuckled and said, 'Come and meet me by the stairs,' and put the phone down.

I met him at the stairs and he laughed at my ridiculous outfit. He told me to go back to my apartment and get changed, and said he would come back and get me in an hour. As I went to leave the club, I explained to everyone I was with that I wouldn't be joining them at the after party. I went back and changed, and touched up my hair and make-up. Then I waited and waited, but he didn't come. I rang his phone but he didn't answer and eventually I realised that he wasn't coming. For the second night in a row, I cried.

On New Year's Day, he began ringing me around lunchtime and got my hopes up by saying he would come and get me in a few hours. This went on all day. By the time evening came, the other girls had decided to have a night in and have room service. They literally ordered every food imaginable. It looked like fun and part of me wanted to stay and join them, but not as much as I wanted to see Mr Starship.

I put on the really tight silver bandage dress and silver shoes I had planned to wear the night before, and waited and waited. I thought he wasn't coming and I was sitting there starving, surrounded by food when he finally turned up. He told me to come downstairs and he took me out for dinner. We went to a lovely restaurant – I can't remember what it was called – and we just chatted all night as we had a lot of catching up to do. I wanted to bring up the times when he had let me down, but, when it came to it, I just didn't want to spoil an otherwise perfect evening.

At the end of the night, we were the only ones left in the

restaurant. I realised I needed to be a strong, confident person for him to want to be with me properly – I'd been mental when we had been together before and I couldn't admit that I was still that person.

I was so happy that I didn't want the night to end, but I was sad at the same time because I was leaving the next day and I didn't want to say goodbye.

We went back to his house and we slept together. Like all the other times before, it was amazing – I knew then there was no way I was ever sleeping with anyone else – but I couldn't stay. My flight was in a few hours and I needed to go back to the apartment and pack.

I was in floods of tears having to say goodbye to him and, for the third night on the trot, I was crying. That concierge must have wondered what on earth was up with me, always crying! I was distraught. I felt like I was walking away from my happiness. I have never cried so much in my life.

I remember sitting on the plane knowing for definite that I was still in love with him – I always had been – and I was convinced that he was The One. I realised there was no way I could risk losing him, and I decided there and then that I would fight for him.

As soon as I arrived back in the UK, I phoned Playboy and told them I would do the last few dates that we had booked in and then that was that – I wasn't doing any more. I then rang Guillaume and broke up with him. He was upset, but things had been fizzling out between us for a while and he must have known that I wasn't into him.

Just a couple of weeks later, I had a call from Layla

Manoochehri – Simon Webbe's girlfriend – who told me that the *TOWIE* producers were trying to get in touch.

Layla and Simon had been in touch with the producers before Series One because Layla really wanted to be on the show. I knew that they had been speaking to producers around the same time as me, but for one reason or another they didn't make it into the show.

Anyway, my friend Ellie who worked for Simon was quite good friends with Layla, so I had met her several times and we always got on OK. Although we weren't that close, we were friends and had spent a fair amount of time together.

Layla gave me the number and I rang a lady called Katie Fox. She told me that they were introducing new characters for the second series and they were seeing people who hadn't made it into the first one. They called me in for a meeting in Holborn, central London. After various meetings and two months of uncertainty, I filmed my first scenes in March 2011.

But, while I made it on to the show, Layla didn't and she was very jealous. She proved just how much a few months later.

CHAPTER TWELVE

Moving On

So, the big day dawned of my first *TOWIE* episode being screened in March 2011. I knew things would change, but I had no idea how much. Neither Joey nor I realised what was about to happen, and how massive it would be for us.

Although I had seen the other *TOWIE* girls on the covers of all the magazines, it still didn't seem real that I could be one of them. After all, some characters have come on to the show and not really made much of an impact.

Once I knew I was definitely on the show, I told just a handful of people because I didn't want to make a big deal out of it. After the New Year trip to Miami, I was still speaking to Mr Starship on the phone all the time. I told him about the show and he said well done and wished me luck, but even he didn't realise how big it would be.

That evening, I invited Ellie round to mine to watch it and, as the minutes counted down, I got more and more nervous. When I saw myself come on screen for the first time, I couldn't look! Ellie was sitting in an armchair and I was on the sofa on the other side of the room; I just leapt on to her lap and started burying my face in her shoulder because I didn't want to see myself!

After literally just a few minutes, my phone went totally mad. It just blew up – I had never seen so many messages and calls in such a short space of time. Lucy Mecklenburgh, who I had met on that modelling job a few months earlier and then got to know on set, had told me to set up a Twitter account before my first episode and the whole thing just went crazy. There were calls, texts and Tweets flying all over the place.

And that's when the Twitter abuse started. The insults came flooding in and, although Ellie was telling me not to read them, I couldn't help it – I needed to see what the public's reaction was.

There it was for all to see – they had picked up on all the things I hated about myself, like my teeth, which stick out because I refused to wear a brace when I was a teenager. I had already been bullied badly enough at school and called 'Space Man' – if I'd worn braces as well, it would have been so much worse.

I've always hated my facial profile because of my lips and here were people I had never even met calling me 'goofy', 'duck' and 'rubber lips'. Then there were others saying I was ugly and plastic, and looked like a man in drag. It was awful – all I could think was: 'The public hate me.'

I have always had a distinctive face so I knew I would get recognised, but naively I thought I would be able to disguise myself, but I can't. Everywhere I go, people recognise me and, while I'm not complaining, it would be nice if I could just switch it off every now and again when I'm having a bad day.

That night, I was terrified I had made the wrong decision; there wasn't just me, I had Mady to think about as well. I was so scared and was worried about people finding out where I lived. Some of the Twitter abuse was so bad that I was scared for mine and Mady's safety.

The next morning, I had to get up and take Mady to school as usual and was dreading it. I never felt like I fitted in with the other school mums, but, that day after the *TOWIE* episode, it was really awkward.

I was standing there in the playground and they were all just staring at me and then looking away and whispering. I was so embarrassed and was dreading the next episode. Mr Starship was great throughout the whole thing, telling me, 'Fuck the haters – it doesn't matter what they think.' I was so grateful for his support.

The team at *TOWIE* were also really good to me. They supported me and did more for me than they really had to. One of the executive producers on the show really took me and Joey under his wing. His name was Gyles Neville and he looked a bit like Hugh Grant. He was tall, with dark hair and with a slim build; also well spoken, with a slight awkwardness about him. He came from a totally different background to us: he had been to university, was a family man and like an

English gentleman, and there he was, dealing with a group of uneducated people from Essex.

I remember filming my first scene at Amy's Salon and he was with me outside. I was so nervous. He put his coat round me and his calm voice really put me at ease. Gyles became like a father figure on the show and helped me through some really hard times, but he left after Series Four and I was gutted to see him go.

There was also the executive producer, whose name was Shirley Jones. Shirley was higher up than Gyles and really attractive. When I first met her, I was a little bit scared of this strong, powerful woman. She has blonde hair, an immaculate dress sense (unlike a lot of people who work behind the scenes in television) and a 'no-bullshit' way about her. I soon came to realise she has a heart of gold and through my dark times we realised we had a lot more in common than I first thought. Even though we are from completely different worlds and have different personalities, Shirley has been a rock to me throughout the show.

Another member of the production team who has become a very good friend is Mike Spencer. You will often see the cast, including me, having jokes with him on Twitter. Most of the cast are very close to him as it's his job to know every detail of our lives. Not only is he great at his job, but he is also very caring and always goes above and beyond the call of duty. Mike has now left the show after Series Six and we were all gutted to see him go. I suppose everyone has to move on, though, and I really wish him the best for the future. I know we will remain friends for a long time.

The production team were all really good to me during those early months. The press gave me a hard time in the beginning as well. They jumped on the fact I'd had surgery. I think they just didn't like the new faces to start off with.

As time went on, I became more relaxed and started getting really close to Lauren Pope. She has been a fantastic friend to me over the past twelve months – I really don't know what I would have done without her.

There is no one on the show I don't get on with, but Lauren and me are especially close. I think, because we are both a bit older than the other girls, we just have more in common maybe. When I first met Lauren, I thought, like most people, that she was quiet and shy, but she is hands-down one of the funniest people I have ever met. She has me laughing out loud every time I see her.

Lauren has helped me through some really dark times and I have found myself confiding in her a lot and spending more time with her than my actual friends outside of *TOWIE*. She's a really good listener and has a real positive attitude. Also, being in a show like *TOWIE*, it's hard for people to understand the ups and downs unless you are on it. We kind of have the same life at the moment and we go through the same experiences – we're almost like an old married couple. We film together, we work together outside of the show and we socialise together. We also go on holiday together – which is a real test of a friendship – and we never argue, which says a lot. There is no negativity in our friendship. Whatever happens, she is a friend for life.

The whole of the *TOWIE* cast are great – no one is fake –

and I haven't disliked anyone from the production company, Lime Pictures, either.

Obviously, I am really close to Frankie and Joey because they are my cousins and, as a family, we all stick together. I have known them both since the day they were born and we have been through a lot together. They have completely different personalities. Frankie has a very strong character but, deep down, she is very emotional. She's turning into a woman in front of my eyes, which makes me feel old. I used to change her nappies! She is really kind, warm hearted and family orientated. Frankie is more like a sister to me, and we argue like sisters, which is fine, but if anyone else tries to argue with her or me then we're the first to defend each other. Both Frankie and Joey treat me like an older sister and confide in me about everything.

Joey embodies the phrase 'what you see is what you get'. He's like a little angel. He isn't a liar or a cheater, and he wears his heart on his sleeve. Joey is more like me in personality and I can safely say we have never had an argument. I have watched him turn into a man since we both joined *TOWIE*. I'm so proud of him and it's unusual for cousins to get on as well as we do. As soon as I go anywhere near him, I start laughing – he's so funny and exactly the same as you see him on telly. He is actually funnier than you see on camera and, when we stop filming, the jokes don't stop.

Lauren Goodger is also a lovely girl but I think she is misunderstood. She is a big diva but not in a bad way – you have to appreciate her personality to understand her. She's funny but she gets taken the wrong way and maybe comes across as rude when she really isn't – she's a genuine, nice girl. When I first joined the cast, she was a bit standoffish but she is fine now.

James 'Arg' Argent can be a bit self-absorbed, but he always means well. When I first joined and he was going out with Lydia Bright, they were really kind to me. They went out of their way to make me feel welcome.

Other than Lauren G, the only other person I didn't warm to straight away was Gemma Collins. Again, she is similar to Lauren; she is someone you need to get to know before appreciating who she really is. I get on really well with Gemma now – I suppose we have the whole 'searching for the love of our life' thing in common. She's looking to settle down and so am I, and we are both determined it will be with the love of our life and we won't accept anything less than perfect. Gemma is really funny and I can sit there and laugh with her. Out of everybody on the show, her personality has stayed the same since day one.

Other people I am close to on the show are the Wright family. Since my very first day, they have treated Mady and me like one of their own. They are a close family unit and exactly how you would imagine a family. Jessica, her mum Carol and her Nanny Pat are all genuinely nice people, and I spend a lot of time with them while filming.

Then there's Joey's best friend, James 'Diags' Bennewith. He is very loyal to Joey. He has had a very hard life, not that anyone would know it, because he doesn't feel sorry for himself or let others know. He's a close family friend and has been for many years. He also has a little brother, who we have renamed 'Baby Diags'. It's funny because he wasn't called Diags before *TOWIE*!

I could go on and on with this list as all the cast members have become friends and they have been amazing people to work with, and I hope everyone goes on to have massive success, on and off the show.

Over the years, I have often found that I don't always click with people straight away, so maybe they think I'm standoffish. Also, everyone always says I look totally different in real life – those are the two things I know people will say. Wherever I go, I always get recognised and everyone I meet always says the same two things!

When I first started on *TOWIE*, I found it really hard to be my natural self when the cameras were around and, although I got used to it quite quickly, it was still nerve-wracking. There is no wardrobe provided: we all just wear our own clothes. They will tell us what sort of occasion it is and we just wear whatever we think. I have always found choosing what to wear really exciting.

There is no hair and make-up either – we all just do our own. In the beginning, I had no idea about the make-up and just wore what I'd usually wear, but I quickly realised that make-up for telly is totally different to normal stuff. Luckily, all the other girls were on hand to give me advice, and now I only wear MAC make-up and I have all the right brushes. I quickly learned all the tricks.

At the beginning, it was hard because I didn't have much cash apart from some savings from my Playboy earnings. Life on *TOWIE* is not as easy as people think. So much hard work goes into making the show. I often get told on Twitter to get a real job, but I'd like to point out that I probably do double the amount of hours many people do in a normal post. I am constantly busy, either preparing for filming or actually filming. Sometimes we film for 12 hours. Filming aside, I have to make money outside of the show so I am travelling up and down the country doing personal appearances, photoshoots and interviews, as well as being a full-time single mum.

We only get expenses to be on the show – a set amount for each day we film, which covers things such as food and petrol to get ourselves to the filming locations – but there is no fixed salary as such. So, for the first few weeks of filming that was all I had earned and I needed to buy new clothes and make-up. Any other money we make comes from personal appearances, photoshoots, interviews and royalties from merchandise.

Everyone is always interested in the way *TOWIE* works and whether or not it's real. I can honestly say that what happens is 100 per cent real. There is no script – nothing is scripted and it is all natural. It is just the situations that are set up – and they have to be, to make sure everyone's stories are entwined.

The job of the researchers is to get to know everything that's going on in our lives. They will bombard us with questions about all sorts of stuff and they literally know everything about us: what we think and how we feel. Basically, we pour our hearts out to them and they put it in the show!

Before filming, they will ask us what has been going on in our lives and then they will pick out the interesting bits and see how they link together with what's going on in the lives of the other cast. And that's how all our reactions are always real – we never know what the other person is going to say. The producers manage to keep that naturalness by never telling us what's going to be said.

During filming, we are all kept separately so arguments can't happen – so it's like a boxing match when we are put together and that's why it makes such brilliant TV.

There are so many people involved in making the show – literally hundreds – and it's like one big family. Everyone knows how it works and there are no haters – but it does get hard because for every series there are new researchers and the producers have changed several times as well.

Each time, we bond with the new researchers because they know everything about us and then, when the next series starts, we often have to bond with a whole load of new people, which can sometimes be hard.

The first few months of me being on *TOWIE* were a real rollercoaster. First, I was branded ugly and that was bad enough. Then the topless pictures previously shot with Unleashed Digital picture agency came back to haunt me. They were on the cover of *Nuts* magazine and over a double-page spread inside as well, which was something I couldn't have dreamed of years before. At first, I was a bit annoyed as I thought I wasn't going to get paid. I rang Craig Johnson-Pass who owned the company, who I had first met at the shoot all those years earlier. I was ranting and screaming, but he quickly calmed me down and explained that of course I would be getting paid. I didn't know that was how it worked. At the time, another photographer was trying to sell pictures of me that I didn't want to come out and Craig helped me out by getting them stopped.

We got on great and I ended up signing up to be managed by the other company he owns, Unleashed PR. I had already met Craig and his business partner, Emma Hadley, at that photoshoot and we had mutual friends, so I knew I could trust them. Emma is very intelligent and direct. First impressions, she could seem a bit hard, but really she's a nice, kind-hearted girl.

Craig, on the other hand, is the complete opposite and we hit it off immediately. He's instantly likeable, someone you would be friends with straight away. He is very open and very approachable; he also does more than his job and we have become more than just agent and client – we are close friends. We speak a lot and he is great at his job. It helps that we can be honest with each other. Often when we work together, it's more fun than work – apart from when he gets back into work mode and wakes me up at 6am for flights home from PAs! He always keeps a positive and professional attitude, even when I don't.

Then the *News of the World* ran a story saying I had never worked for Playboy. They had rung Playboy in America, who said they had never heard of me. So, of course, I looked like a liar. I had never said I worked for Playboy in America: I worked in France and that was totally separate. It's like ringing up McDonald's in America and asking if they had heard of someone who worked at McDonald's in England – well, of course, they wouldn't have heard of them! They didn't bother to put a call in to me, ITV or my agent. Journalists should always ring up someone when a story is about to come out to check if it's factually correct and, also, to give you a right to reply; they didn't bother. I felt helpless and I had no voice; I had no idea how to react to it. This was my first taste of the downside of being in the public eye.

So now I'm ugly and I'm a liar. That was bad enough, and then Simon Webbe's ex-girlfriend, Layla Manoochehri, betrayed me in a way I had never imagined. We had been friends. My best friend Ellie was friends with her so I knew her and we had got on. And then she went and sold a story on me.

A couple of years earlier, a few of us had been on a night out – me, Ellie, Simon and some others – and Ellie and me had gone back to Simon's to carry on drinking at the end of the night. Anyway, we'd been talking about cooking and I was saying, although I'm not a great cook, I can make an amazing shepherd's pie. Simon said that was his favourite dish so Ellie nominated me to make this for Sunday lunch for everyone; I'd go round the next day and cook for them all.

I was drunk at the time and it was just something that was said, and I thought it would all be forgotten, but the next day he rang Ellie to remind us that I was going to be cooking for them. I was so hungover it was last thing I wanted to do. Even though I knew there was nothing in it, I said to Ellie, 'Mr Starship will go mad,' but after much deliberation I reluctantly decided to do it as Simon had treated us to the night out. I mean, what could go wrong? It was only a shepherd's pie! I went to the supermarket, bought all the ingredients and took them round to his house with Ellie, and cooked it for him and his friend. I spent the whole time in the kitchen, cooking. Then

I dished it up, stayed for about two minutes to eat a little bit of it and left. That was it.

The following morning, I was lying in bed with Mr Starship when suddenly there was a knock at the door. As I went to answer it, I saw Layla walking back to her car and thought she must have been looking for Ellie. Ellie was Simon's PA, but Layla was under the impression that Ellie worked for her too and was always asking her to do things for her.

I rang Ellie and told her Layla had been round, and I presumed she must be looking for her. Ellie explained that Layla had gone mental because she had seen the shepherd's pie dish and questioned Simon about it. That was understandable, but it was completely innocent and I thought Layla knew me well enough at that point to know I wasn't interested in Simon.

Both Simon and Layla knew about the love of my life. I rang Layla immediately, but she didn't answer. I left her a strong voicemail explaining that in Essex going to someone's doorstep to confront them is not how things work but she didn't come back. She later claimed that she threw the pie at me, but there wasn't even any left, and anyway I didn't get the dish back for a further four months!

After a while, it all went back to normal and, as far as I was concerned, the shepherd's pie incident had been forgotten. Layla never brought it up so I thought she knew she had overreacted. We all carried on socialising together as usual and there was no problem in my eyes.

One night, a few months later, we were all out at Nu Bar in Loughton. Layla was there too and she was fine with me. As far as I was concerned, there was no problem with us. We even posed for loads of photos, one of her kissing me on the lips, like girls do on a night out. Hardly the actions of someone even remotely annoyed with me!

There were loads of people out and at the end of the night Simon invited everyone back to his place. As well as Simon, Layla, me and Ellie, actor Gary Lucy, who used to be in *Hollyoaks*, was there too and some others, including Jaime, Simon's best friend, who had been to Manchester with us a few years earlier. She had been in a band called VS (which were managed by Simon) and had been going out with Marvin Humes, who was in the band with her and is now in JLS.

Anyway, Jaime and Marvin had recently split up. She was gutted and had moved in with Simon and Layla for a bit to sort herself out. So, me, Jaime and Ellie were all sitting in her room, chatting and drinking.

The whole house was full – you couldn't walk into a room without at least five people being in there. This was a normal weekend occurrence for Simon and Layla; they were always throwing parties. Then Simon and Gary Lucy came in, and we were all just sitting there talking. It got pretty late and I'd had a lot to drink – I've always been a bit of a lightweight – so I was lying in Jaime's bed half asleep, listening to everyone chatting when all of a sudden Layla came in and went mental.

I was lying on the bed and Simon was sitting on the end of it, and that was it. I mean, I was fully clothed, lying on the bed, and Simon was fully clothed and sitting on top of the covers! Layla even lied later on that I was wearing a white dress. In fact, I was wearing a white one-shoulder top and wide leg jeans! It was totally innocent. And anyway we weren't alone – the others were still in the room as well.

But she went mad, crying and shouting and I just thought, 'I don't need this – get me out of here!' I was begging someone to get me out of there because I was drunk and half asleep, and all I could think was: 'Leave me out of all this! I do not need to be caught up in one of their regular childish arguments.'

I just wanted to get out of there – fast. Jaime, who has known Simon since they were kids and as I've said was living there at the time, didn't want to stay either. So, we got a taxi and she stayed at mine.

The whole thing was a lot of fuss over nothing, but even after that everything went back to normal with Layla and me, and the night wasn't mentioned again. I put it down to her being drunk, and I had seen her several times after that – she even took Mady out for dinner with Ellie just before I went on *TOWIE*. If she had any sort of problem with me, there was no way I would have let her take my daughter out for dinner.

Then, at the end of March 2011, just weeks after I'd started on *TOWIE*, Simon invited me out for his birthday. He and Layla had split by this point.

His birthday party was at Funky Buddha and I wore a short, tight black dress with 'The Champ' written on the front. It was a great, but crazy night. I was papped by the paparazzi! I couldn't believe it – they were calling out my name and I was shaking with nerves. As I walked into the club, people were pointing and saying, 'There's Chloe from *TOWIE*' – it was mad!

Layla wasn't invited as Simon was now dating a new girl called Maria Kouka, but she sent Simon a text, saying: 'You think you're clever not inviting me. Watch what I do next.'

A few days later, Craig received a phone call about a story the *Mirror* were planning to run – they were saying that Layla had caught us in bed together. She said we were in her and Simon's bedroom – which we weren't – and that I was on top of him and he had his shirt off. It was just ridiculous – I was practically asleep so there was no way I was on top of him! Craig rang me and at first I laughed as it was so ridiculous, but then I felt a sense of dread – I knew from the Playboy story that the public believe everything they read. Craig informed the paper it was completely incorrect; ITV and Lime were also great and all tried to get it stopped. They explained to the paper exactly what had happened and even put them in touch with witnesses, who were there at the time.

I was so upset; I begged Simon to try to fight it, but he wouldn't. He thought that, if he just let it lie, she would stop but, if he stopped the story, who knew what she would do next? To my horror, a week later, the story ran. I was advised not to comment by ITV – it would continue the whole saga for a few weeks. Also, I was frustrated, as I was in love with Mr Starship but couldn't announce this publicly as I wanted to keep our relationship private.

Let me get one thing straight: I do not fancy and have *never* fancied Simon. He's just a friend. He is totally not my type – he's a lovely guy who has helped me out but I couldn't go out with him in a million years and he knows that. I couldn't go out with a guy who writes songs and sings for a living – it's not manly enough for me! I don't fancy him at all.

But this story was blaming me for their break-up. There were loads of lies and it was horrible.

I couldn't believe she could do that to me. She was a friend of mine, and she knew I didn't want Simon; she also knew how much in love I was with Mr Starship. Simon was her fella, and I wasn't interested in him.

Nothing went on that night, but Mr Starship didn't believe me that it was all a pack of lies and he still thinks something went on now.

Layla knew how hard I'd had it and then she tried to ruin everything for me out of sheer spite. She was brought up like a princess, with a mum and dad who spoilt her rotten. Everything was handed to her on a plate. But really she didn't do herself any favours. Essex is a small place, and everyone knows everyone else, and a lot of people were angry at what she had done, but there is one rule: no one likes a grass. She was effectively hounded out of the county and, as far as I know, she's gone back to Birmingham (where she's from). I guess Layla wanted her five minutes of fame from this story, which never happened. I mean, they didn't even use her picture in the article – they used a photo of Jaime by mistake!

During the time that I knew Layla, she had been on *The X Factor* as part of a girl band (also called Girlband) and I had supported her while she was on the show. They didn't do too well, though, and she later gave up on her singing career. She then appeared on the reality show *The Bachelor*, but she didn't do well on that either.

So, after her story, I'm now an ugly, home-wrecking liar and I'm still worried I've made the biggest mistake of my life.

Luckily, though, things soon got better. I started getting closer to the other stars of the show, as well as the production crew.

I was offered my first ever photoshoot and interview with *Star* magazine. I had to go to the *Express* building in central London and I was really nervous, but my agent, Craig, calmed my nerves. They wanted me to re-create the famous Dita Von Teese pose in a Martini glass. The glass was so big it couldn't fit in the studio, so I had to do the pictures in the underground car park. I kept slipping on all the bubbles and I was shaking because it was so hard to hold myself up!

It was mental. There I was, sitting in this giant glass in just my underwear, when I had another 'how on earth did I get here?' moment. It was mad!

Around this time, I was also offered work doing personal appearances but I was too nervous to do them for the first few months. I found it hard knowing who to trust and it was all so new to me.

At the beginning of May 2011, I went to see Mr Starship when filming for Series Two had ended. We had been speaking virtually every day and I couldn't wait to see him.

He hadn't realised how famous I was back in the UK until I was recognised by British tourists in Miami. He was shocked the first time someone came up to me, asking to have their photo taken with me, but he was really proud of me. By this point, I was used to being recognised, but it was one thing being spotted in Essex and another thing entirely when it happened in a totally different country.

Meeting up with Mr Starship again was another roller-coaster of emotions. I was so happy about seeing him again, but he still wasn't being the same with me as he had been when we were first together. The magic was still there between us, but we hadn't seen each other for such a long time so we had a lot of catching up to do.

When it came to leaving him, I was distraught; I didn't want to go home. I cried all the way to the airport and all the way through security, and all the way back on the plane! As soon as I got back to the UK, I just wanted to go and see him again.

Frankie and me had planned to go to Marbella at the end of May for the usual Bank Holiday weekend and had been really looking forward to it. Ellie was coming, too, and was really excited. She was skint so I'd offered to pay for her as a thank you for all those times she had been such a good friend and pulled me through my darkest days.

My agent had arranged that I would do a photoshoot while I was out there. It was all booked and we knew we'd have a great time because loads of the other *TOWIE* cast were going, too.

The day before we were due to leave, I went to a clothes shop in Loughton called Bonnie and Clyde to get some things for the trip. I know the girl who works in there so we were standing there, having a chat, when her mum came out from the back. Her mum is a psychic and she took one look at me and said, 'You look really tired.' She told me to go into the back and sit down with her, so I did.

It was so strange. She said to me, 'You're in love with

someone who lives in a different country and you think he's going to change, but he never will.'

I couldn't believe it! I burst into tears; I was so drained. I'd finally got Mr Starship back in my life after all our time apart. I'd just been out to see him, then had to leave him and I still had no idea how serious things were between us. Since the trip earlier that month, I'd cried at some point every day over him and it was awful.

Still sobbing, I ran out of the shop and rang him. I told him what the woman had said. I was so upset. But he was so calm; he just said, 'Why are you listening to a stranger? She doesn't know anything. I am flying you out here tomorrow.'

I was in shock. He had never offered to fly me out there before, and more than anything I wanted to just get on a plane and go to him. But I was going to Marbella the next day and I couldn't let my friends down, or my agent. I rang Ellie and told her the whole story, and she was amazing. She is the only one who understands how I feel about Mr Starship. She told me to go to Marbella, do the photoshoot as agreed and then fly out to see him.

Frankie wasn't so understanding and was none too impressed, nor was Joey, but I didn't care: I just needed to see Mr Starship. So I changed my return flight and Mr Starship booked me on a flight to Miami and rang me to give me all the details.

I went to Marbella, did all my photos in one day, even crammed in a quick personal appearance, and then raced back to the airport. I landed back at Gatwick, got in a taxi to Heathrow and caught my flight to Miami.

It was a lovely trip and I fell even more in love with him. I was infatuated but I still felt he wasn't giving me his all. Any mention of us being boyfriend and girlfriend and he would just clam up. In a way, it was even more torture than not having him at all: I had him back and I knew 100 per cent that he was The One for me, but I couldn't make him go back to the way he was in the beginning. I was trying not to act too desperate because I thought that would make it worse, but it was torture.

Again, I cried all the way home. The customs people must have been thinking, 'Here she comes with her big eyelashes, crying all over the place again.'

Although it was awful leaving him, I had to get on with my life and I was excited because I had planned another boob job in June.

I had never really been happy with my first boob job because I had wanted them in front of the muscle, but Mr Starship said no. I had gone along with having them behind the muscle to please him, but I'd never been totally happy. They were too high and they had never dropped because they were behind the muscle; I wanted a more natural look and, if they'd been in front, they would have dropped a bit. Until I started on *TOWIE*, I didn't have the money to have them done again, but, as soon as I landed a part, I booked in for a consultation.

This time, I went to see a top surgeon at the Welbeck Hospital in London called Dr Miles Berry. I told him I wanted to go in front the muscle but he explained that I couldn't do that because my skin was too thin at the front. I was gutted that I couldn't get what I wanted, but there was nothing they could do. I put my foot down and said, 'No, that's what I want,' but being such a great surgeon he argued with me and said he couldn't do it. Dr Berry could have taken advantage of the fact that I was in the public eye and just done what I asked in return for publicity, but he didn't and stuck by his professional word. I was grateful for how genuine he was.

I still managed to have the implants replaced and went up to a 34E. I had wanted to go even bigger, but I couldn't. Because of the skin being so thin, the surgeon said you would literally have been able to see the implant through it. After already having had one boob job, I was more worried than before about the surgery and any complications, but I was pleased with the results.

In August, I arranged to meet Mr Starship in Marbella. That was when he realised just how famous I had become. We are both very private people when it comes to our relationship, so we didn't want to get papped together, which was hard as half the *TOWIE* cast were in Marbella and it was paparazzi central. The public all thought I was single, even though I really wanted to scream from the rooftops, 'I'm in love,' and tell everyone how wonderful he is, but our relationship is too precious and I will do anything to keep it that way.

Being on *TOWIE* is an amazing experience, but I often felt bad as I wanted Mr Starship more and would have walked away from it had he told me to. Like I said at the beginning of this book, I never set out to be famous and it wasn't my dream: it just happened. My dream is still the same to this day – to finally be with the love of my life. I had to do it, though, for Mady; I had to make the most of this amazing opportunity I'd been given for her sake.

My heart has always belonged to Mr Starship but I knew I needed to prove to him that I want him for him. I'm not interested in anything other than him. Over the years, people have tried to ruin our relationship. Some girls think their liaisons with him will change my feelings. I'd like to point out nobody can change my mind about him: this is real love.

Any way, I can honestly say I had the most amazing few days in Marbella with Mr Starship. It was action packed and we didn't sleep much. I don't like wasting a minute in his company. As our romantic trip came to an end, Mr Starship reassured me and told me not to be sad. He said he loved me and wanted to marry me, and we would be together soon. When we were in the airport waiting for our flight in the bar, I went to reapply my lip-gloss. As I went to open my bag, to my surprise, there was a box. A bottle of Chloe perfume was sitting there. I was so surprised! God knows how he managed to get it in there without me seeing. My eyes welled up! It wasn't the perfume it was the thought, and the way he always surprised me.

I came back from Marbella content, but we still weren't properly back together.

Filming began on Series Three and the time flew by. Before I knew it, we were rapidly approaching November and my 30th birthday. Frankie and I decided I should do something totally different, so we organised a wedding-themed 30th birthday party – on national television! All my life, I had hoped I would be married by the time I was 30, and by then I was wondering if I would ever have that fairytale wedding of my dreams, so I decided I would have one – but without a groom.

Joey was my best man and Mady was my bridesmaid, although she hadn't been shown on screen at that point because I wasn't sure I wanted that for her: it felt like a big decision to make and I wasn't ready to put her under that kind of scrutiny. It was all very well people slating me, I could handle it, but I couldn't deal with anyone saying stuff about Mady. I had Frankie, Lauren Pope and Lauren Goodger as my bridesmaids – it was the best birthday party I'd ever had!

I had a wedding cake, cupcakes, a horse and carriage, wedding food and even received wedding presents. Frankie got a wedding book made for me and made sure everyone there put a birthday/wedding message in there. I will treasure that book forever.

On top of that, I had all my *TOWIE* cast mates there, the whole crew, my friends that I have known for years and my entire family. It was amazing! Joey even wrote a speech and did the first dance with me. Frankie really put herself out and organised a lot of it for me. She made it so special, and it meant a lot.

Now things were pretty much back on track with Mr Starship, I really hoped he would fly home for my birthday but, as the day grew nearer, I realised he wouldn't be able to make it due to other commitments. Even during filming, I'd be thinking about him. I'd be standing there, thinking, 'I don't want to be here, I just want to be with him,' the whole time. I needed to try to appreciate the opportunity I'd been given, but I found it hard.

On the morning of my big day, he still hadn't called and I was beginning to think he'd forgotten. Then Frankie turned up on my doorstep, holding a box, and told me it was a present from Mr Starship. I was all confused. She explained she had rung him to remind him about my birthday and he had put some money in her account and told her to go and buy me a pair of Louboutin shoes.

They were classic black peep-toe shoes and I loved them as soon as I saw them, although when I tried to walk in them I wondered why everyone was so keen on them, they were agony! I was over the moon he had bought me such a lovely present and he rang me to wish me 'Happy Birthday'. I hadn't heard from him earlier as he didn't want to call until I had received my surprise.

But then I didn't hear from him for five days and it drove me mad. I thought I would lose him again and I couldn't stand it. I had lost him before, and I was so paranoid and insecure about it happening again.

I was so upset and angry that when he did get in touch I was yelling, 'You can't just disappear!'

He was so calm; he just said, 'Yes, I can – you can't tell me what to do.'

He is such a free spirit; he never makes plans and it drives me mad. I want to put a time limit on everything and know exactly when I will see him again, but he just lives day to day.

After those five days when I didn't hear from him, I decided enough was enough. I couldn't live my life like that. Why was I putting myself through it? Every time I had to say goodbye, I had to suffer the same dread that I might never hear from him again. Each time I went to visit, I never got any answers from him about the future. Even though he still talked about us getting married one day, he would never even say he was my boyfriend. On the other hand, he always told me he loved me. He had never once said, 'It's over' or 'I'm not in love with you', so I always had hope. At least if he said that, maybe I would have been able to move on.

So, I made a pact with myself. This was getting ridiculous: if he was serious about me then he would spend Christmas Day 2011 with me. And, if he didn't, that would be it. I felt like I was putting my whole life on hold for him. My flat was freezing as there was no heating downstairs and I really needed to move, but I kept on thinking there was no point, because I was always waiting for Mr Starship to ring and ask me to move to Miami with him. I was just waiting around for him to commit to me properly and I couldn't carry on like that; I was adamant, if he wasn't with me on Christmas Day, that was that – it would be over for good.

Meanwhile, things on *TOWIE* were getting better and better. The producers rang up and offered me the chance to go to Lapland for a Christmas special. I was really flattered to have been asked. They were only taking five of us – Joey, Lauren Pope, Lauren Goodger, Mario Falcone and me. There was uproar among the original cast because us new ones had been picked.

We went for four days in mid-December and I shared a cabin with Joey, which was a right laugh. He had me giggling the whole time. The log cabins we stayed in were really nice and the five of us all got on really well, and really bonded on that trip. I hated Lapland. It was freezing cold and the food was disgusting – there was no way I was eating reindeer meat!

The day before we were due to fly home, Mr Starship rang me. He asked me where I was, and I told him I was in Lapland.

'Why didn't you tell me?' he said.

'Because I haven't heard from you,' was my reply.

Then he dropped a bombshell – he was standing outside my flat! For two years, I had fantasised about him turning up on my doorstep and surprising me, and when we does I'm in bloody Lapland, freezing my tits off. Typical!

He was annoyed with me because I hadn't told him I was going away and I was wrong-footed because he had done a really nice thing for me. Cold and miserable, I hated Lapland even more after that. It wasn't Christmassy at all and I just wanted to get home.

I was excited because I knew Mr Starship was in London and I guessed that meant he would be staying for the whole of Christmas so maybe I would see him on Christmas Day after all! But a week after arriving home I hadn't seen him and I was getting impatient, but I still hoped we would be spending Christmas together.

I had gone into central London Christmas shopping and I was in Selfridges, buying Mr Starship's present, when my phone rang. It was him. 'Where are you?' he asked. I told him I was in Selfridges and he said, 'So am I.'

I couldn't believe it! I didn't know whether he was winding me up or not. I didn't want to bump into him because I was casually dressed, with hardly any make-up on, so I ran out of the shop and back to my car, put some high heels on and re-applied my make-up. I was going out in London that night so I had a pair of heels in my car ready to change into, as well as my make-up bag so I could re-apply before the evening.

Then I ran back to where I'd been before and carried on shopping. He rang again and I told him I was in the men's department, and he said he would come and find me. The next minute, there he was, walking towards me. It was like something out of a film. I was so happy to see him. All the pain I'd been feeling just went straight out of the window.

I looked at him and I just thought, 'Oh my God, I love him!' He was so familiar and yet the sight of him took my breath away.

He took me for champagne and it was like being in a dream. But I had to go – I was meeting my dad. We had decided that we would go for dinner and see a show instead of buying each other presents. I was taking him to Nobu because he'd never been there before and I was really looking forward to treating him after everything he's done for me. And then he was taking me to see *Ghost: The Musical* for my present. I'd been really excited about it.

But now I was with Mr Starship, and I know it sounds awful, but I didn't want to go and meet my dad. It seemed as though one of us always had to leave. We said goodbye and Mr Starship said we could meet up later on. It spoilt the whole evening with my dad, really

After I had dropped my dad back home, I rang Mr Starship but he didn't answer.

The next time I heard from him was the day before Christmas

Eve. Frankie, Lauren Pope and me had decided we would have our own sophisticated work night out, just the three of us. We went for dinner in Nobu and were having a lovely evening when my phone rang. It was him, wanting to know where I was. I told him I was having dinner and he said he would come and find me. He asked me what time they stopped serving and said he would definitely be there.

But he didn't come. I was on edge for the rest of the evening, waiting for him, but he never came. When the restaurant closed, Lauren suggested we go to the Hoxton Pony, in Shoreditch, east London, where a group of her friends were partying.

That was when Mr Starship rang again. I told him we had left Nobu and were at the Hoxton Pony. He said he'd come, but I didn't think he would. Then, as if by magic, he arrived. I had pined for him, cried over him and there he was. I was so happy! Frankie and me were doing happy dances when he wasn't looking.

From the minute I saw him, I was back in our little bubble. Everything else was a blur. I thought that was it – we would definitely be spending Christmas Day together. Already it was the early hours of Christmas Eve.

It got later and later, and the bar closed and it ended up being just us lot and Lauren. We were all pretty drunk by that point.

The paparazzi had followed us there and were outside waiting for us to leave. There was no way I wanted to get papped with Mr Starship so we decided that he would go out of the front door and I would leave via the fire exit at the back, then we would meet round the corner.

So off he went out of the front door and, a few minutes later, I went to leave out of the back. But when I got outside all the paps spotted me and came running over, so I tried to run back inside. But the paps were trying to get in as well. I managed to get back in and the manager went to slam the fire door, but he trapped my finger and literally slammed it in the door.

It was like a dream. I was screaming, but no sound was coming out. The pain was like nothing I have experienced before – it was worse than childbirth.

Luckily, Frankie noticed and started kicking the doors, trying to get them open. The pain was excruciating but all I could think about was Mr Starship. He would be waiting for me round the corner, wondering where I was but my phone battery had died.

Eventually, I managed to get my finger free and someone called for an ambulance. The tip of my finger had snapped in half, it was triple the size and there was blood everywhere! Everyone was really worried, but all I cared about was my ruined night with Mr Starship.

This was not supposed to happen. I had our romantic Christmas all planned and this was a disaster. My life was meant to be all glam and glitzy now I was on the telly, but here I was, in the early hours of Christmas Eve, in total agony after yet another drama. And once again, I found myself thinking, 'Why does nothing ever go right for me?'

CHAPTER THIRTEEN

The Course of True Love Never Runs Smoothly

The paramedics gave me gas and air for the pain and I was taken to University College Hospital, near Euston. Frankie came with me in the ambulance and was brilliant. They gave me a pain-relief injection, but told me I needed to see a hand doctor and there wasn't one there, so I was taken to the Royal Free Hospital in Hampstead, northwest London.

By this time, it was morning. I hadn't had any sleep and I was still in agony. My dress was covered in blood and I was so upset. I asked for more pain relief and they gave me another injection, but they weren't happy about it because apparently no one gets two.

I always do my food shopping in Marks & Spencer on Christmas Eve and I had my whole day planned. Although I was going to my dad's for Christmas dinner, I wanted to get loads of nice nibbles and treats for Mady and me. I also wanted to get a small turkey so that I could have sandwiches and feel festive.

It got to 1pm and I knew there was no way I would make it to the shops in time. At 1.15pm, on Christmas Eve, I was finally seen. I was really upset because I'd wanted it to be perfect. I had made such a big effort to enjoy this Christmas. I was so organised; I had all my presents wrapped and hidden, and I'd even decorated my front room and got a new TV, as well as new decorations for the tree. I was adamant this Christmas wouldn't be like any before, and I just wanted to get home.

I told one of the doctors that I couldn't sit there, and he was really nasty and said, 'Just because you're on telly, you won't be getting special treatment.'

I couldn't believe it! He told me I would need to go into theatre to have my nail surgically removed but there were no free theatre slots that day and I might have to come back the following day. There was no way I was going back into hospital on Christmas Day! This hospital was an hour and a half away and it would have taken at least a few hours to perform the treatment, so it would have taken up the whole of my Christmas Day.

Eventually, I went in to see the consultant and, luckily, he was much nicer than the other doctor. I told him I just needed to get out of there – I'd been up all night, I'd had no sleep and I just wanted to go home. I think he must have felt sorry for me because he agreed to remove my nail right there and then. He also had to do some reconstructive work on my finger to ensure the nail would grow back. Little did I know that I would still be waiting for it to grow back fully eight months later.

It was horrific – I have never felt pain like it. Frankie was nearly passing out! He gave me a glass of water while he bandaged it up and then the other horrible doctor walked in. He took one look at me sitting there like a princess, having got my own way, and gave me a proper filthy look.

I was so relieved to get out of there. Frankie asked the hospital to order a taxi as we both had no battery in our phones at that point and no one knew where we were. I was so relieved to be out of there, as I knew I had so much to do at home. As soon as they bandaged my finger, I ran out without even picking up my extra painkillers.

That was my Christmas pretty much ruined. I couldn't drive and I was in agony. I'd had no sleep and the painkillers they had given me previously were making me even more tired.

When I got back, my phone battery was still dead. I rang Mady's grandparents off the landline and explained what had happened and how much pain I was in. They offered to keep Mady overnight, but I had never woken up on Christmas Day without her so I told them to drop her back a few hours later. I then rang my dad to explain what had happened and he rushed straight over. I told him that I couldn't drive and I had no food for Mady and no painkillers; also, I was in agony as the anaesthetic had worn off. He told me to write down a list of everything I needed and he would go and get it. I told him not to, but he insisted and he rushed off to Waitrose. He got as much as he could but most things were sold out because by now it was 4pm on Christmas Eve.

When my dad left, I was in so much agony and, as I had barely slept, I was exhausted so I decided to try to get a few hours' sleep before Mady came home from her grandparents. I could barely sleep as I was in so much pain and having to keep my hand elevated.

Mady came home and she was so excited, we stayed up and watched telly on the sofa in front of the tree. I felt terrible as she was excited while I was physically exhausted and in agony. That night out had ruined my whole Christmas.

Frankie told me she had rung Mr Starship from the ambulance to tell him what had happened, but he hadn't come back. She was really pissed off with him: she knew that he could hear me screaming in pain in the background but he still didn't come back. I was so out of it I didn't even know she had called him.

I hadn't heard from him since but then my phone rang. He asked if I was OK. I explained what had happened and he said he didn't realise it was that bad. He stayed on the phone for a good half an hour. He ended the call saying he would ring me straight back as he was getting in his car – but he didn't.

I put Mady to sleep and then quietly tried to get the presents out from where I'd hidden them in a cupboard and put them under the tree. I was in absolute agony and I had to hold my finger upright, meaning I was doing everything one-handed – I had to move a six-foot Christmas tree and drag all the presents out without waking up Mady. I also had to make sure all the little things were in place for the morning: I arranged the cookie, milk and carrot to make it look like Santa had been.

When I finally collapsed into bed, I was exhausted. I couldn't wait to get to sleep as my finger was causing me so much pain. The next thing I knew, I was woken up by Mady being sick in the bed. I couldn't believe it! My first thought was: 'Is someone kidding me?' I had to get up, wash her, change her pyjamas, change all the bed sheets, get rid of the sick smell and put fresh sheets on her bed – all with one hand.

I woke up and I was so tired, and in so much pain. I just wanted to go back to bed and cry and sleep, but I had to make the best of it for Mady. She was so excited. We'd been out and bought all new decorations and had spent hours decorating the tree and getting all prepared. Matthew came over and gave her the present he had brought with him. He wasn't very sympathetic about my injured finger – I don't think he appreciated how much pain I was in and how awkward it was only being able to use one hand. He stayed for about half an hour and then the three of us went for a coffee.

All year, I had worked so hard to try to achieve something so that Mady and me could have a fantastic Christmas. I was gutted. I woke up on Christmas morning determined to make the best of it, but I couldn't even open any presents because of my finger.

Frankie came and picked Mady and me up and took us to my dad's. Although I had told everyone Mr Starship might be coming for Christmas Day, he didn't turn up.

I was upset and angry. I felt humiliated in front of my family because they were all asking me where he was and I had to say I didn't know. I didn't want everyone to know how upset I was, so I put a brave face on it all the way through dinner. I made the most of Christmas, and, in the end, I had a lovely day. My dad had bought Mady a professional Karaoke kit and I enjoyed playing with it more than she did. The whole family kept begging me to stop singing as they were getting a headache, but it kept my mind off my throbbing finger!

Another year had gone by and Mr Starship and me still weren't together at Christmas. I was devastated, but I couldn't let on how upset I was. I'd wasted another year of my life trying to make it work. I'd gone out of my way to go over and see him, which wasn't cheap. Every time I was spending about £600 on flights, which was an added expense.

That evening, Frankie and me made some turkey sandwiches and went back to my house. I was so upset and angry, and I knew I needed to stick to my guns. I'd been adamant that, if Mr Starship didn't spend Christmas Day with me, then it meant he wasn't serious about our relationship and it was over.

So, I sent him a text. It said: 'You've let me down again. I am starting the New Year fresh without you. You have no need to contact me again. Goodbye.' And that was it. I know it might sound a bit harsh, but I felt strong and adamant that I must stick to my decision.

On Boxing Day, Mady was spending the day with her dad and I was meant to go to Lauren Goodger's for a girly day, as she had just moved into a new place and had invited me over. All I wanted to do was lie in bed and sulk. Tired and in pain,

I couldn't drive anyway, so I decided to stay at home and feel sorry for myself.

Later that day, Mr Starship started calling and texting me but I just ignored him. I had made my decision and I knew I needed to stick to it. It was too late. He kept on calling but I just let it go to voicemail – I had no intention of talking to him. In my head, Christmas was over and he was a day late. He didn't even ring me on the day to wish me Happy Christmas.

That night, I had been booked to do a personal appearance with James 'Arg' Argent at a nightclub in north London and I really didn't want to go, but it was work. I didn't feel up to it and even getting ready was a struggle because I couldn't use my finger. It took me ages to get my false eyelashes in. Everything was made more difficult because of the stupid bandage.

Arg is always late for everything and this was no exception: he arrived two hours late to pick me up. We drove to the club – Opera House in Tottenham – and it was packed. My head was pounding and I just wanted to be in bed. I remember standing there, thinking, 'What am I doing here?'

The following day, Mady was coming back from her grandparents and I decided it was time to pull myself together and stop moping. I'd had my day of sulking but now I needed to put a brave face on it all for my daughter. Because of all the drama with my finger, there was literally no food in the house and I needed to go shopping.

I had no make-up on and I was wearing an old black velour tracksuit and Ugg boots, but I didn't care. Mady and me walked around the corner to my car and set off for the shops. She switched the radio on and the first song that came on was 'Hungry Eyes' from *Dirty Dancing*. That song has always reminded me of Mr Starship and I wondered if it was a sign, but then I remembered the pact I had made with myself and put it out of my mind.

We went to the supermarket and got all our goodies, and then set off back to the flat. Halfway home, I spotted a flash car in the rear-view mirror and suddenly a thought flashed into my mind: 'Could that be Mr Starship?' Then I told myself to stop being silly. I always used to fantasise that would happen when I saw other cars. It was silly – of course, it wouldn't be him, I told myself, especially after the text I'd sent. I carried on driving, but the car kept following me. Every time I turned a corner, it would do the same. As I came to the road where I had to park, it was still behind me and I remember thinking, if it pulled into the parking bays, then the driver was definitely following me.

I told Mady to get out of the car, and we grabbed our bags and went to walk off when the window on the other car lowered and my heart stopped: it was Mr Starship. I was so shocked. He had come to find me! My heart soared. Then I remembered I had to be strong and stick to my guns, so I just blanked him and went to walk off. By this point, he was out of his car walking towards me. Plus, I looked a right state and didn't want him to see me like that! So I just said, 'I've got nothing to say to you. You've let me down,' then walked off.

Unfortunately, Mady had other ideas and went running over

to give him a hug, then asked him in for a cup of tea. I couldn't believe it! So we all started walking around the corner to the flat and he was being all sweet to her. As soon as we got inside, Mady was showing him her Christmas presents and they were having a great time. Mr Starship has always been really good with Mady ever since we first met back in 2007 when she was just a toddler. Plus, he used to stay over all the time so Mady was comfortable around him. She has a real soft spot for him, too, and was really excited to see him.

Mr Starship told me he really wanted to talk and asked if we could go for a drink. He seemed genuinely sorry. So, I asked my neighbour, who was also a good friend, if she would look after Mady for an hour for me. She said yes, so off we went in his car to the King William pub in Chigwell.

He told me he had been really busy and that he hadn't even seen his own family on Christmas Day because he was so manic. It was a really crucial time for his business and that, if I would just give him three months, then things would be better. He promised we would spend New Year's Eve together. I was touched that he had made a big gesture and put himself out to come all the way to see me, so I agreed to give him another chance. He had told me what I wanted to hear, and I was relieved that it wasn't all over.

Again, he had to leave because he was flying off somewhere, so off he went, promising he would call me to arrange New Year's Eve. Although we spoke on the phone several times, nothing definite was arranged.

It got to New Year's Eve, and he rang me and said, 'Where are you? Why aren't you here?'

I was fuming. He hadn't told me to book flights! How could he just assume I would be going over to see him?

So there I was, with no plans and I was furious. There was no way I was sitting in! I had vowed to stop wallowing, and I wanted to see the New Year in on a positive note. I knew the manager of the Cafe de Paris in London's Leicester Square so I called him and he said that he would sort me out a table for three friends and me: Ellie, Krystal, the make-up artist, and her friend. I got myself all glammed up and even gave my bandage a vajazzle by sticking diamantes all over it!

By this point, it was nearly the evening and I knew it would be virtually impossible to get a taxi into central London so I decided we would catch the tube as there was a Central Line station at the end of my road. What a terrible idea! It is really not advisable for a reality TV star to get on a tube train on New Year's Eve. The train was packed and everyone was drunk and in high spirits, and people wouldn't leave me alone. I felt so intimidated. I always try to stop for fans, but, when there are about a hundred of them screaming and shouting things out under the influence of alcohol, it's scary!

It turned out to be a good night; the manager had laid on drinks and the four of us had a dance and a bit of a giggle.

Mr Starship sent me a text at midnight, something he hadn't done for years, but I didn't reply as I still had the hump. When it was time to leave the club, we tried to get a cab home, but there were literally no taxis anywhere. We decided we would have to brave the tube again. It seemed everyone in London had the same idea: the tube was so packed that we couldn't even get into the station, there were security guards at the top stopping people. It was freezing cold and I just wanted to get home. So we sweet-talked the security guard into letting us sneak through a no-entry to the tube platform. He told us his daughters were big fans of *TOWIE* but didn't have a clue who I was. He took my word for it and I assured him I was definitely in the show. I had my picture taken with him, told him to show his daughters in the morning and he agreed to escort us down to the platform.

We finally got on a tube and again it was packed full of people, most of them hammered. I should have been somewhere fabulous, seeing in the New Year with the love of my life, not stuck on a tube full of drunks! I don't get on the tube on a normal day, let alone New Year's Eve. I had been determined that this Christmas and New Year would be great, but again they hadn't lived up to my expectations.

On New Year's Day, I decided Mady and me needed a holiday, so I rang my friend Ellie and asked if she would like to come with us. She jumped at the chance. I decided we would go to Miami. Mr Starship wasn't there at that point, but it was somewhere I was familiar with. I knew my way around and I knew the weather would be good. Plus, I knew Mady would love it over there. Ellie came over and we were just looking at flights when Frankie turned up. She said she was desperate for a holiday, too, and so we booked it for the four of us. We were due to go a week later and I couldn't wait.

Mr Starship rang me and asked what I was doing. I told him I had booked to go to Miami and he dropped the bombshell that he was flying back there in a few days' time so he would be there when we arrived. He said he really wanted to spend time with me – just the two of us – so I arranged that I would fly out for three days on my own and then Ellie and Frankie would bring Mady out to me. It was all sorted when the *TOWIE* producers dropped another bombshell: they needed me to film an advert for the upcoming series while I was away.

So, I ended up flying out for three days, then flying back through the night and going straight on to film the ad. Then I went to pick up Mady and meet the others, and flew back through the night again. I spent two nights sleeping on a plane and, when I finally arrived back, I didn't know if I was coming or going!

The trip was perfect. I forgot everything bad that had happened. Mr Starship was amazing and we were closer than ever. We stayed at his house and he made a real effort. He had been shopping and cooked us meals. It gave me a real taste of what it would be like if Mady and me lived there with him. Mady had the trip of a lifetime, too: she swam with dolphins and just loved being there.

I was devastated to be leaving, but I had to come back for filming and Mady needed to go back to school. I just wanted to move over there and live happily ever after.

For the first time in ages, we discussed our future. He told me that he thought it was important for me to finish what I'd started in the UK and I agreed. We would think about being together properly at the end of 2012. For now, we decided to keep things how they were. In the meantime, we would see each other as often as we could between filming. And then, at the end of the year, we'd hopefully be together.

I knew in my head that he was right. I needed to make sure I was financially stable in case it didn't work out. I had to have something to fall back on for Mady's sake, as well as my own, but in my heart I just wanted to stay there and forget about everything else.

Yet again, I cried all the way home and this time Mr Starship seemed really upset that I was leaving, too. It's almost as if he forgets he loves me when we're apart but, when we're together, he remembers and then he's gutted when we have to say goodbye. When I first get home, he calls me all the time and is always telling me how much he misses me, but, as time goes by, the calls become less frequent.

So, I went back and started filming for Series Four and I got through it. Halfway through the series, Mr Starship came back to the UK and we ended up having a stupid row. He rang me one night to tell me he was in Movida with some of his friends and asked me to go and meet him. Movida now has a rule that reality TV stars aren't allowed in, so I told him I couldn't go there. He asked me to go and pick them up, so I did. I drove them all back to my flat and me and him went to bed.

The next morning, I woke up to find that his friends had drunk a huge magnum of champagne that I'd been given as a gift on my 30th birthday from Mick and Kirk Norcross. I'd been saving it for a special occasion and I was fuming. I was also annoyed with him for bringing his friends back with us, but he apologised and everything was fine. A few days later, he had to fly back to Miami and so off he went again.

Then, in mid-February we had another massive row and

everything went wrong again, even though it was over something really minor.

I was filming a scene with James 'Diags' Bennewith, where I was giving him skincare advice. When we are filming, obviously we can't have our phones with us. On that day, I had my phone on the side out of sight of the cameras but I could see it flashing with a message. I have my phone set up so that, when Mr Starship messages, it flashes pink. I could see it flashing and flashing away, but as I was mid-scene there was nothing I could do. I kept on seeing it flash, so as soon as the scene was finished I rushed home so that I could Skype him. I remember feeling really stressed because I wanted to get home as quickly as I could.

When we finally spoke, he was in a mood because I hadn't answered his messages. I was annoyed because it wasn't my fault but he kept picking on me and it was like he was trying to start an argument. I started getting angry because I'd rushed home and then he was being off with me, so I told him, 'I can't talk to you when you're like this,' and I hung up on him! Literally, I just cut him off the Skype, which was something I'd never done before.

After that, he didn't speak to me for nearly three months! I couldn't believe it. We completely fell out over that incident. As time went by, and he still wouldn't speak to me, I got more and more angry that he had let me down again over something so small.

I decided enough was enough. I was waiting around for him and not living my life. While I was living my life around him, what was *he* doing? He certainly wasn't living his life around me.

I'd been skint for so long that I was scared to spend any of the money I was earning. By now, I was so used to living on virtually no money that I couldn't bring myself to splash out, but I needed to be properly settled and to move out of that flat on the Queens Road in Buckhurst Hill. I was fed up with the noise and not being able to park outside my own place. Every time I wanted to leave the flat, I had to trek miles to my car and, because it was a busy high street, I had to face the public every time as well. There were often paparazzi hanging around because *TOWIE* stars Lauren Goodger and Billi Mucklow have their salons along the same road.

I found a house and, as soon as I saw it, I fell in love: it was perfect. It was far away from any main roads, had a lovely garden and its own driveway. Also, it was down a cul-de-sac so there would never be any reason for people to be walking past. After two-and-a-half years of traipsing to my car, I couldn't wait to park it just yards from my own front door.

It had just been renovated and totally redecorated, and everything was brand new – fresh paint, new carpets, the lot. But it was more than I wanted to pay and I was worried about spending so much more. Then the estate agent told me they had other people interested so I just went for it and signed the lease.

I also needed a new car. Six months earlier, I'd been leased a Mercedes, which I wasn't that keen on, and by this point I was fed up with it. I wanted a car of my own, so I splashed out on a beautiful white Mercedes. I love it!

Then came another big decision: I was going to have a bum lift. I wanted to get full-on bum implants but everyone talked me out of it because it's a major operation and you literally can't sit down for weeks after. I had always hated my flat granny bottom and I really wanted to have it done, but my friends and family persuaded me to have a less invasive bum-lift treatment, which involves injecting your bum with your own fat.

Basically, they removed fat from my stomach and thighs with a syringe. It felt like a rod going under my skin and was very painful. Then they emptied the fat into a hospital drip bag to separate and drain it before injecting it back into me.

The procedure was really painful and the results weren't even that great – I wished I'd gone for the proper bum implants in the first place. I'd been through all the pain but had nothing to show for it, so later this year I'm going to have another procedure. I tried the subtle route and it was *too* subtle. I've already had a consultation, so watch this space!

As my life always seems like one long drama, the next big event was just around the corner. The day after I'd had the bum lift, I was lying at home feeling sorry for myself when I had a phone call from *Reveal* magazine. I was doing a weekly column for them at the time and they rang to tell me they had been sent an email from someone claiming to be my mum.

I was totally shocked. I couldn't believe it! I'd been expecting her to get in touch as soon as I went on *TOWIE*, but by this point I had been on the show for a year. Why on earth had she chosen now to get in touch?

The girl at the magazine said she would forward the email on to me at home. I was still drowsy from the drugs they had given me, but I wanted to see what she had to say for herself.

'Hi Chloe, I'm your birth mother,' she had written. She went on to say how she had so much to tell me, so much more than she could fit on an email. She said she had twins and that my sisters looked just like me (she didn't say whether they were both girls or one girl and one boy, though). To prove that she was my real mum, she had put details in there, including her real name, my dad's name and mentioned my Nanny Linda and my Nanny Daisy – things she couldn't have otherwise known – so I knew it was definitely her. She told me to contact her on Facebook.

It was so weird reading her email. I didn't feel anything – all I could think was that the spelling and grammar were awful. Some of it took me ages to decipher because it was in text-message-style abbreviations. I kept thinking, if you were sending an important email like that to the daughter you hadn't seen for nearly 30 years, surely you would make more of an effort and take time over it.

I decided that I couldn't deal with it that day. After all, I'd just had an operation. So I left it for a few days. But I kept on thinking about her, so I logged on to Facebook and typed her name in. It came up with a long list of people, all with the same name, and I didn't know which one was her, so I started scrolling down and looking at the pictures but I still didn't know which was the right one. I'd be staring at a picture, thinking, 'Is that her?' I'd seen a picture of her at the age of 20 and now she'd be 50, so I had no idea what she looked like.

And then it hit me: she was a total stranger. I didn't even

know what she looked like. What was I doing? I was looking at pictures of a bunch of strangers and trying to work out which one was my mum.

I suddenly thought, 'I'll never meet you,' and that was that. Anyway, what good would it do if we were in contact? I've managed 30 years without her and here I am, surrounded by people who love me. I didn't reply to her email and I have made no effort to contact her. And I never will: I don't need her in my life.

Her email made no mention of Mady and the fact that she is a grandma. It was all about *her* kids. And I know it sounds cynical but I just thought she was contacting me to test the waters before she told her family about me. Or that she was thinking of her own kids and what I might be able to do for them as their famous sister.

It didn't seem to be about me or my interests and so that was it. I told my dad, my best friend Ellie and later Mr Starship, and that was it. I decided there was no point telling anyone else.

After all that drama, I decided I needed a break, so Lauren Pope and me booked a girly holiday to Los Angeles for the beginning of April. I had never been before but I'd always wanted to go. One of the girls I had been on the Ibiza trip with years earlier was a mutual friend of Lauren and me. She was already over there and had told us she would look after us and get us into all the best clubs.

We were due to fly three days after I moved house and the following few weeks were totally manic. I packed up all my stuff and was ready to leave the flat but then, on the day I was due to move, I suddenly thought, 'What am I doing? Why on earth am I moving three days before I go away?' I'd put myself under too much pressure. I started panicking and stressing, so I rang my dad and he got a van and helped me move – I couldn't have done it without him. I then had three days to unpack as many boxes as possible and then pack for my trip. I was also worried about leaving Mady for a week, but she would be staying with my Nanny Linda for some of it and then her grandparents for the rest of it, so she was really excited, too. By the time I got to the airport, I was exhausted.

As soon as Lauren and me boarded that plane, the excitement took over. I literally couldn't wait! We flew with Air New Zealand and they upgraded us to first class. It was amazing – I had never been in first class before and I couldn't believe how good it was. We were treated like royalty. It was like being a proper celebrity. Lauren and me were so excited, we were happy clapping! We had proper beds, we could choose our food from an actual menu, like in a restaurant, and they had tablecloths and proper cutlery.

For the first time in months, I felt myself beginning to relax. I was so exhausted it was good to be on a plane with nothing to do apart from eat nice food, drink champagne and watch movies – although we couldn't really eat much of the food because we wanted to be as skinny as possible for LA!

When we landed, we planned to go straight to our hotel, get showered and changed, then go straight out. We only had six nights there and we didn't want to waste a single one. Lauren and me were really close at this point, and I felt really comfortable with her because she's so laid-back.

We collected our cases – which were massive and contained easily enough clothes for at least a month – and headed through customs. Lauren had already warned me that she might get stopped by immigration because she had experienced problems once before. They had thought she wanted to work there and questioned her, but it had all been resolved.

This time, she was stopped again and taken off into a room by one of the officials. By this point, I was desperate for a cigarette because we had been on the plane for 12 hours, so I told her I would go for a cigarette and come straight back. As I was walking through the arrivals hall, I heard someone shouting, 'Miss, Miss!' behind me. I didn't think they were talking to me so I carried on walking. Then, all of a sudden, a customs official stopped me and told me I had to go back with her. She took me back and made me wait with Lauren.

No one would tell us what was going on and I was getting really annoyed because I wanted a cigarette and I also wanted to get out of there. Lauren was telling me to keep quiet and just take it because getting stroppy would only make things worse, but I was livid. We had been treated like royalty on the flight and now we were being treated like scumbags!

After three hours, they finally came out and decided to go through our suitcases. They literally took out every single piece of clothing and shook it, and then just chucked it back in again. Everything in my case was neatly folded and packed because I'm a bit OCD when it comes to packing, and seeing them making a mess of my lovely things made me even more angry. Once they had been through every single item in our cases, they told us we were free to go. There was still no explanation as to why we had been kept there.

I had been really looking forward to the trip to LA: it had started off so well with the flight but immigration officials had ruined our first night. As we left the airport, we saw some paparazzi photographers who were British and recognised us from *TOWIE*. They were really nice and even offered us a lift to our hotel!

We had chosen to stay at the Mondrian in Hollywood, which is really posh and famous for its rooftop pool and the Sky Bar. When we arrived, we were told that both the pool and the bar were closed for renovation and would be shut for the whole time we were there. It was all going wrong! We had pictured ourselves sunbathing up there and were gutted. The staff were really apologetic and even offered to upgrade us to a suite to make up for it, though, so it wasn't all bad.

Despite being exhausted, we decided we would still go out that night because we didn't want to waste a single night of our holiday. Plus, I was just so excited and couldn't wait to get out and see LA. So we got ready and headed out to a club called Greystones in West Hollywood – we'd heard it was one of the trendiest clubs. But when we got there it turned out to be a house music club and I hate that kind of music. I ended up getting paralytic – I think it was partly because of the jet lag and the tiredness – and, after a few hours, we went back to our hotel.

The next morning, Lauren went into organiser mode and literally planned out every minute of the rest of our trip. She's a proper organiser! Because I have to be responsible when I have Mady, as soon as I'm not with her, I just give up totally and let other people take charge. We went to Santa Monica and spent a fortune in Victoria's Secrets – we both bought loads.

Although I was loving LA, it was making me miss Mr Starship. Everything about America was associated with the trips I had made to see him out there. I kept seeing people driving the same car he drives and little things like that.

For the five years I have known him, he has always worn the same aftershave, which you can only buy in the States or in Harrods. As Lauren and me were walking past a perfume shop, I spotted it in the window, so I went in and bought it. I didn't tell Lauren it was Mr Starship's aftershave, I just said I wanted to buy it. I sprayed it on me and it was like being with him. It ended up making me even more upset – I don't know why I bought it in the first place! I wished I hadn't because it just made me miss him more. I wanted to be strong, though, and not contact him.

That evening, we went to the opening of a restaurant and managed to arrive just after Jennifer Lopez and Arnold Schwarzenegger had left! But we did see Cat Deeley and Mario Lopez, who played A.C. Slater in the US teen sitcom *Saved By The Bell*! Although we were looked after, it was quite weird not being recognised over there.

We met up with some friends of Lauren's who were over there and afterwards they took us on to this really cool secret club – I don't even know what it was called. It was full of music-type people and I felt totally out of place. I was wearing a mini-dress, with my boobs hanging out, and everyone else in there was wearing T-shirts with pictures of bands on the front and Converse trainers. They were all really cool-looking and I was the total opposite!

The next day, we headed over to Rodeo Drive to do some serious shopping because, even though we had bought enough clothes to last a month, we realised it was all the wrong stuff, so we went out and got more. We also went rollerblading in Venice Beach, which was really good fun.

But the more time I spent out there, the more it made me miss Mr Starship. I had been so determined that I was going to be strong and not contact him, but I just couldn't do it. So, I gave in and texted him. I told him I really missed him. As I sent the text, I literally held my breath, waiting to see if he would reply.

CHAPTER FOURTEEN

Happy Ever After?

After what felt like an eternity, he finally texted back. It was really short and distant but I didn't care – at least he had replied. I knew I could work on him, I was just so grateful we were back in touch. We carried on like that for a while, me texting him telling him I loved him, and him just replying with one-word answers. I told him that I was still in love with him and I couldn't get over him. Although he wasn't saying he missed me, I felt better just being back in touch – I couldn't carry on pretending I was strong enough to move on.

I enjoyed the holiday but I still kept thinking, 'I don't want to be here' – I just wanted to be with Mr Starship.

On our last night in LA, Lauren and me decided we would try to find an R'n'B club because all the clubs seemed to play house music and we were missing that kind of music. The friends we had made took us to this place in Hollywood and it was proper ghetto. I was shitting myself! It was massive and there didn't seem to be any exits apart from one front door. I honestly thought that, if anything had kicked off, I wouldn't have made it out of there alive – it was mental! It was packed and hot, and I've never seen men as big and tall as that before in my life. All I could think was: 'Get me out of here,' so we headed back to a friend's for a house party.

Everyone else was cracking on until the early hours but Lauren and me were like proper old grannies and went back to the hotel, ordered room service and went to bed!

We were due to fly home the following afternoon and had decided to make the most of our last few hours in the sunshine so we headed over to the Roosevelt hotel to use their pool. It was lovely, we lay by the pool drinking Bloody Marys and I felt really relaxed. That's what we had planned to do in our own hotel so the holiday ended on a nice note. We couldn't wait to get back on that plane because the flight over had been so amazing. And it was even better because we could eat all the nice food now we weren't on diets any more!

Filming for Series Five started the day after we got back and we were both totally knackered. Although the next few weeks were completely manic with filming, Mr Starship and me carried on texting each other. As time went by, he became more and more friendly on the texts – he sent me one that said: 'I'm so proud of you. You've done so well.' Things were gradually getting back to normal. Then he told me he missed me and I was over the moon so I sent him one back, asking if that meant we were back together and if he was still my boyfriend. His reply was: 'I never wasn't your boyfriend' and I was instantly happy again.

Series Five finished mid-May 2012 and we had just one week off before it was time to head over to Marbella to film *The Only Way Is Marbs* special. I was desperate to see Mr Starship but I had loads of commitments and only seven days to fit them all in. Plus, I already had to leave Mady for a week for the Marbella trip and I didn't want to leave her again.

Mr Starship was on business in Turkey so I juggled all my commitments and worked out that I could fly over there on the Friday afternoon and then back again on the Saturday afternoon. Mady would be staying with her grandparents so that was all fine. On the Sunday, I had to fly to Spain for a magazine shoot, then fly back ready to go off to Marbs on the Wednesday. It would all be a massive rush but I needed to see him.

I didn't tell anyone I was going because I always feel like people only want to hear about things when they are going badly. No one in particular, I just find other people are never that bothered about things going well. I was still annoyed with Mr Starship for ignoring me for all those months over a petty argument, but I let him think everything was fine, although I planned to have it out with him when I arrived.

After not seeing him for three months, I was so excited and couldn't wait to get there. My flight was delayed and, when I arrived, he texted me to say he was too busy to come and meet me. He texted me the name of the hotel and told me to get a taxi straight there. I was fuming – I'd never been to Turkey before, I had no clue about the currency and I didn't even know where I was going. I'd moved heaven and earth to go and visit him and he couldn't even be bothered to come and pick me up!

The hotel was an hour away in a taxi and the whole way there I was thinking that the taxi driver, who didn't speak a word of English, could have taken me anywhere. I was in a foreign country and, apart from Mr Starship, no one even knew I was there. When I eventually got to his place, I was so relieved. I rang him and he said he would come down and meet me. So there I am sitting in reception and the lift doors keep opening, but it's never him. After a while, he rang and asked me where I was, and it turned out I was in the wrong sodding hotel! It was one with a similar name and the taxi driver had taken me to the wrong one. So now I had to get another taxi to take me to the right one and I was even more angry; if he'd just come and picked me up, this wouldn't have happened.

Suddenly, everything that had annoyed me was to the forefront of my mind and I just thought, 'What am I doing, chasing this man around the world?'

He texted me and told me he would wait for me in the bar. He said, 'I've got a drink for you. You sound like you need it,' and when I finally walked into the right hotel I saw him straight away. All the anger and hurt just melted away – he looked so handsome. He saw me and smiled, and that was it. I really wanted to have a go at him but all I could think was: 'I love you.'

Then he told me we were going for dinner with a big group of his friends and that I didn't have time to get changed. I was hot and bothered from the journey and I had all my outfits planned. The one I was wearing was my arrival outfit, not my going-out-for-dinner one! I ran up to the room and quickly got changed into the tightest, sexiest dress I had. It was really tight and made me look like a bottle of Jean Paul Gaultier perfume!

There was no time to bring up any of the stuff that had annoyed me and then we were in a packed restaurant and I was tipsy, so I just forgot all about it – I didn't want to spoil it. I hadn't met any of the friends he was with before, but they were all really nice and made me feel really welcome. We ended up going on to a club and didn't get back to the hotel until 6am. I was meant to be leaving at lunchtime to fly home but there was no way I was going anywhere; I was still drunk and hadn't even been to bed. So I rang Craig, my agent, and told him I had missed my flight. Luckily, he was really good about it, but he told me I absolutely had to come back the following day and I promised him I would.

Mr Starship and me spent the whole day lying in bed snoozing, watching films and ordering up room service. After all the rushing around, it was so nice just to relax and chill out together; I was so happy. That evening, we went out for dinner and once again ended up in a club until the early hours. This time I wasn't as drunk because I knew there was no way I could miss that flight!

As I was getting ready to leave for the airport, Mr Starship was half asleep and, as I went to go, he grabbed my hand and said, 'Don't go.' I was crying as I said goodbye. I couldn't believe I was walking away again, but I had commitments. I was going to Spain for a cover shoot for the *Sunday Mirror*'s *Celebs Magazine*, which was a big deal for me. The flight out was due to leave just a few hours after I landed back from Turkey so I didn't even have time to go home. My agent was coming with me, as well as Mady because I didn't want to be away from her any longer. So he collected Mady and they met me at the airport.

We went to grab a coffee before we boarded the plane and I was so tired after another night of no sleep and upset at leaving Mr Starship that I left my iPad on the side in Costa Coffee. But I didn't realise until we were at the gate and about to get on the plane, and I was distraught: it had been a present from Mr Starship so it had massive sentimental value. Plus, it was our way of keeping in touch with each other on Skype. I went running back through the airport but it wasn't where I'd left it. Although I retraced all my steps, it was nowhere to be seen. I asked security but they were really unhelpful and, anyway, we were about to miss our flight so I had to go.

By this point, I was tired and pissed off; already the trip was turning into a nightmare. I rang Mr Starship, crying, and he told me not to worry and that he would buy me a new iPad, but I was still upset. After another four-hour flight, we finally arrived in Spain, with an hour-long journey to our hotel. When we arrived, it was early evening and the whole team from the *Sunday Mirror* were there. They took us for dinner, so I had to be upbeat. Then I had to sit down and do the interview, which was all about body image, when all I really wanted to do was go to bed.

The following day, we had to be up early to do the photoshoot on the beach. It ended up taking the whole day and it was a lot trickier than they first thought – it was so sunny that I was literally squinting into the camera lens! As soon as they were happy that we were finished, we had to race back to the airport and fly home. I was desperate to get back but the flight was delayed and then my mobile battery died. Now I had no way of contacting Mr Starship, and I was tired and emotional. When I finally got home, the first thing I did was plug my phone in, but it wouldn't switch on – it had crashed completely.

That was the last straw. I was going to Marbs in two days' time and I needed a phone. I was missing Mr Starship. Plus, I was anxious about leaving Mady for a whole week. I was totally knackered, but I needed to pack for filming the *The Only Way Is Marbs* special episode and get everything sorted. My whole life is one great big rush, I feel.

I spent the next day running around to sort out the clothes I needed, getting my hair done and packing. It was all such a rush. The following morning, we were meant to be meeting at Southend Airport so we could film, but I was late. I hadn't had time to get ready so I ended up jumping in the car they sent to collect me without any make-up on. As we drove to the airport, I literally just had time to put my face on!

When I arrived, it was mad – the whole cast were there, as well as the regular tourists and it was really busy. We all piled on to the plane and all the tourists must have thought it was mental being on a plane with literally the entire cast of *TOWIE*! I was sitting with James 'Arg' Argent and he spent most of the flight farting, which was a bit off-putting to say the least.

Once we had landed at Malaga Airport, we all went our separate ways to where we were staying. The producers of the show had offered to put us up in villas, but Lauren Pope and me had decided to stay in a hotel on our own because we thought the villas would be a bit hectic.

We'd booked to stay at a boutique hotel called the Sisu Hotel, which was down by the port and had been recommended to us. Arg was staying there as well – he'd been giving it the big one and had booked a suite – so the three of us, Lauren, Arg and me got a cab there.

By the time we arrived at the hotel, it was around 11pm, but we had decided we would still go out because we were excited and we wanted to make the most of being away. My cousin, Joey Essex, had told me we had to go and meet him at Pangaea Night Club, so Lauren and me went off to unpack and get ready. It took us ages to get sorted and it was nearly 1am when we were finally done. We went down to the hotel reception to book a cab, but they told us there weren't any taxis. How could there be no cabs? We couldn't believe it! So we decided to walk out on to the street to flag one down, but not one would stop for us.

In the end, the chef from the hotel, who had finished for the night, took pity on us and offered to drive us to the club. So Lauren and me piled into his old banger and off we went. The whole way there, we were looking at each other, thinking, 'What are we doing?' – we didn't have a clue where we were going; he could have taken us anywhere!

Luckily, it was all fine and he dropped us off right by the club. As we were walking down the street, an English man came running up to us covered in blood, saying he had been stabbed. He asked us to call him an ambulance. I don't know why he stopped us – we were in a foreign country and we didn't know what to do. We helped him to a taxi rank because we didn't have a clue how to phone for an ambulance. We made sure he got into a taxi safely and that the driver would take him straight to hospital. We wanted to help, and advised him to phone the police, but we didn't really know what more we could do. Anyway, we were so shocked that we felt a bit freaked out by it – there was so much blood and his attacker could have been anywhere.

We carried on our way to Pangaea but, when we got there, everyone was drunk – Joey, his girlfriend Sam Faiers, her sister Billie, Tom Pearce, James 'Diags' Bennewith, Arg – and it was really packed in there. Lauren and me still felt a bit on edge, so we decided to go off to a different club, which was quieter and we ended up having a great night. We had loads of drinks and didn't get back to the hotel until about 7am!

The next day, we had a day off filming, so we headed to our hotel pool and my cousin Frankie Essex and some of the other *TOWIE* girls – Lauren Goodger, Cara Kilbey and Billi Mucklow – came and joined us. It was a great day – we got two white leather beds by the pool and spent the whole day drinking and throwing each other into the swimming pool!

The following day was the day of the famous Champagne Spray Party – where I had first met Calum Best all those years earlier – and it was a full-on day's filming. We started filming at lunchtime and literally didn't finish until about 4am the following morning. People kept throwing me in the pool, which was a nightmare because I didn't want my hair ruined! We were filming and I wanted to look my best, but it was so hot that we were sweating our make-up and fake tan off. Although it was a long, exhausting day, it was brilliant fun too.

The rest of the trip was a whirlwind of filming and partying – the whole week was such a good laugh. We ended up hanging around in a gang that consisted of six girls – Lauren P, Lauren G, Frankie, Cara, Billi and me – and three lads – Joey, Diags and Tom Pearce. Everyone got on really well and I had the best time ever – I felt like I was 18 again! I really made the most of it and properly enjoyed myself.

Then, on the last day of the trip, something even better happened – Mr Starship texted me and told me that he loved me. It was the first time he had said it since we made up after falling out earlier in the year. I told him that, when I got back to the UK, I had five weeks off until filming for Series Six started in July. He said that he was going to be on business in Europe but he would arrange for me to go out and meet him. I was so excited!

As we left Marbs, we were literally all ruined – we were exhausted from all the partying and the drinking and late nights. I was so excited about seeing Mady again. I'd been away from her for a whole week – a long time for me – and I just wanted to go home, give her a big cuddle and then have a really long sleep!

Over the next few weeks, I was in constant touch with Mr

Starship and he kept saying he would arrange for me to go and meet him. I packed my case so that I would be ready to go at the last minute and I called my best friend Ellie, who had said she would look after Mady for me whenever I needed. Every day, I would speak to Mr Starship and he would say that he was waiting for the right opportunity when he wouldn't be too busy and we would be able to spend some quality time together but, as the days and then weeks passed, I was getting more and more impatient.

I was busy doing my own work of photoshoots and interviews but I was still trying to arrange it all so that I could go out and see Mr Starship when he called. As time went on, I grew more and more frustrated.

It was also getting embarrassing because Ellie kept asking me when I was going and my family kept asking what was going on as well. It had been going on since the day I came back from Marbs and I hadn't made plans to do anything else because I was waiting for his call. All the other *TOWIE* cast had been making the most of the break and had been away on holiday but I'd been sitting at home, waiting for Mr Starship! I was scared to take a holiday in case I missed him. I could have taken Mady away and I was really annoyed. I kept on thinking that he could have made time, and the more he kept me waiting, the more furious I became. But I really wanted to see him – I needed to sort out what was going on between us once and for all. He had messed me around long enough and I wanted proper answers and proper reassurances about the future.

Finally, the week before filming was due to start again, he

rang and told me he would be in Ibiza that Wednesday and to book my flight. I had to be back for filming on the Monday, so we would have five days together. It wasn't great, but it was better than nothing. So I booked my flight, called Ellie and got myself ready. I was just sorting out my final bits when he sent me a message to say I couldn't go that day – I had to wait until the Saturday.

I was furious. That would give us only one day and one night together. I'd had a whole five weeks to see him and yet I would end up seeing him for just one day! So, I told him no. 'What's the point?' I said (I had to be back on the Monday for filming). He told me I should just come back late and, for a little while, I actually considered it but then I realised I could get into big trouble and for what? It wasn't worth it. He wasn't risking anything for me, so why should I risk everything for him? I couldn't mess up my work because, after him and Mady and my family, work is the most important thing I've got. So I told him no way! I went mad – I'd had no holiday and I was desperate to sort things out with him. I needed to speak to him, and I wanted to do it face to face but it wasn't going to happen so I cancelled my flight. I was so annoyed that I unpacked my case and put it all away.

The next day, he rang and told me he'd be getting to Ibiza on the Friday night and begged me to change my mind. So I re-booked my flight and ran around like a mad woman, getting everything organised. As it was the weekend, Mady would be with her grandparents, so that was all sorted. I rang Ellie and asked her to give me a lift to the airport and somehow I was ready in time. I was excited and nervous, but

I made it. The flight left Luton quite late and it was like a party – everyone seemed to be already drunk and I felt totally out of place. I ended up sitting with these two guys who struck up a conversation with me about *TOWIE* and were really nice. When the drinks trolley came, I ordered myself a vodka and managed to relax a bit.

When we landed in Ibiza, the airport was packed and I couldn't see Mr Starship anywhere so I headed outside to wait. Then he rang me and said, 'Where are you?' He'd been waiting for me in the arrivals hall but I'd missed him because it was so busy. He said he would come and find me, so I quickly unzipped my case to try to find my make-up and then, all of a sudden, there he was. He was standing there looking ridiculously handsome while I was sitting on the floor, with the contents of my suitcase sprawled out on the pavement!

Just like every time I see him, it was amazing and I was literally speechless. It was already really late but he drove us back to the hotel and told me to get ready so we could go out. I quickly changed into my best dress which was a tight, black bandage dress, and we headed out to a club called Leo's. They were playing house music which neither of us knew but we didn't care. We had a few shots and were drunk pretty quickly, then we just danced the night away. Mr Starship made friends with one of the waitresses who just kept bringing us drinks and it was a brilliant night. Everyone was wearing these ridiculous neon glasses, so he asked her to get us a pair each. They were like geek spectacles. His were pink and mine were yellow but I had to pop the lenses out of mine because they wouldn't fit with my false eyelashes!

Although there was so much I wanted to say to him, I didn't want to ruin our night, so I waited until we got back to the hotel and then I just blurted it out. All the anger, the hurt and the frustration came tumbling out. I was in a rage crying because I was drunk and emotional. The next morning, I woke up and realised I must have passed out during our row because I had no idea what he had said in response to everything I'd said. Plus, I was absolutely starving because I had eaten literally nothing the previous day. So we ordered room service and sat on our balcony, which looked right up into the mountains. There was a little white church right on top of the mountain. I pointed towards it and said, 'We could get married there,' because it looked so perfect. He just looked at me and smiled – I think he knew I was only half joking!

We sunbathed by the pool for a bit and then decided to go for a drive. He took me to the old part of Ibiza Town. It was lovely and it felt like being on a real holiday. Because Miami is so posh and exclusive, it never really feels like I'm on holiday when I go over there, but in Ibiza there were souvenir shops and little winding streets, and it felt like we were on a proper holiday together. The old town was really pretty and we walked around for ages before stopping to have an early dinner in a little restaurant. We spent hours sitting there, eating and talking. Again, I decided to bring up everything that was bothering me.

He totally reassured me. 'We will be married one day,' he said and I was so happy. He just doesn't make plans, he explained – he doesn't want to make promises that he can't keep and let me down so he can't make concrete plans. But he told me not to worry about anything: I was the one he wanted to be with, no one else. Happy with what he had said, I decided to drop the whole thing.

When it came to paying the bill, he was signing the credit card slip and I joked that he should use the pen to write me a love letter. He got a business card out, turned it over and started writing on the back but he wouldn't show me what he was writing, which I thought was weird because it was meant for me!

Once we had finished dinner, he said, 'Come on, let's go to that church you saw.'

I thought he was joking, but he wasn't, so off we went up the hill. It took us nearly an hour to get up there, but we did it and it was just so amazing. Of course, it was closed, so there was no chance of actually getting married but it was the most romantic setting I could ever imagine. I was so happy, I can't describe it – the sun was setting and the sky was beautiful. There were a few other tourists up there, so Mr Starship asked one of them to take a picture of us. He doesn't usually do soppy things like that, but he knows I love that kind of thing and I was really touched.

It was the most romantic thing ever and I started to cry. 'What's the matter?' he was saying, but all I could reply was: 'I don't know – I'm just so happy!' I asked him if he thought we would ever go back there again and he said we would. On this trip, he was different somehow – it was like he really wanted to reassure me that we had a future together.

As we walked back down the hill, we passed a bar with tables outside and candles everywhere, and I commented that it looked lovely. So he said we would go in for a drink, even though it was totally empty. We sat at the bar and had a couple of drinks and then it started filling up in there and we found out that a band was playing that night. They were a Spanish band, but they would be singing songs in English. I couldn't believe it when they started singing the first song. It was from the film *Pretty Woman* and it's one of my most favourite songs ever! This was so weird – it was like a sign and it was so romantic I didn't know whether to laugh or cry.

After a few drinks, we were in the mood for a proper night out, so we went back to the hotel and got changed. Whenever I'm with Mr Starship, he always rushes me to get ready and I never have time to do it properly, and this was no exception. We had decided to go into the party resort of San Antonio so that we would go to a club that played music with words rather than house music. He told me not to even bother getting changed because it would be really casual, but I said there was no way I was going out in my beachwear! I put on a cream pencil dress and black Louboutin heels (which in my world is casual), and he just laughed and told me I was way over-dressed. We drove into San Antonio and I realised he was right – I was totally over-dressed. It was packed, people were literally everywhere and half of them were wearing bikinis!

It was heaving, simply packed with people and nowhere to park. There were about 100 mopeds parked and in between them there was a small gap. Mr Starship decided he was going to squeeze in between them! I was laughing so much. I asked, 'What if you knock them over?' He said he didn't care! After showing off his parking skills, people began to notice the flash big car squeezing in between all the bikes and, in turn, they started to notice me. We waited for our chance and legged it to the club.

We had a nice night, though, and were both exhausted when we finally got back to the hotel because it had been such a full-on day. The following morning, I woke up with the familiar feeling of dread because I was flying home that night and I didn't want to leave him. It was Sunday and I had to be back to start filming for Series Six the next day. We had crammed so much into such a short trip that I decided to let Mr Starship sleep in as I knew he was really tired, even though really I didn't want to waste any of our time together. I crept around getting ready and then headed to the pool to sunbathe, but, as soon as I got myself settled and ordered a Bloody Mary – my favourite holiday drink – he rang and told me he would come down and find me.

I could see him on the balcony of our room and I didn't want to be away from him for another minute, so I got my things together and went back up. He wanted to go to the Blue Marlin Beach party so I put on a white bikini with a nice white beach dress and a pair of red wedges, and piled my hair into a bun. We decided to have lunch by the pool first and, by the time we arrived at the beach club, it was already busy. Heading straight for the bar, we ordered some cold drinks and stood and chatted. I was feeling sad because I had to leave but I put it to the back of my mind and for the next three hours we just laughed, totally lost in our own world. People surrounding us were like a blur.

Eventually, we had to leave there and we went back to the

room to pack before heading for a final meal. I was sad but trying to be strong and, once everything was packed, I slipped on a tight black dress, freshened up my make-up, took one last look at the room and view, then off we went. Mr Starship had told me about a restaurant he had accidentally found on one of his first ever trips to Ibiza many years earlier; he said it was a little romantic place and that he always thought he would go back there one day. He asked the concierge to find the address and then put my luggage in his car and away we sped. He's so funny like that, so brave – he didn't know his way around that well, but he will persevere until he gets to where he wants to be. Somehow he found the restaurant that he had been to once about 15 years before. It was perfect, white like a little church, and inside was very pretty and small, decorated in traditional Spanish decor. We chose a table and sat down for our last meal together, and, although I was tearful at dinner, it was really nice.

After we finished the meal, we sat and talked for a while. I was heartbroken at the thought of not seeing him for five weeks while I was filming the next series of *TOWIE* – the weekend had been so perfect and romantic, I was gutted. He drove me to the airport, with me trying not to cry. When it was time to say goodbye, we had a big cuddle and I held him so tight, it was killing me to let him go. He asked me if I was OK and if I would be all right. Somehow managing a watery smile, I said yes, I would be OK. He got back into his car and watched me as I walked to the entrance to the airport. Before strolling through the doors, I turned and waved, then he pulled away. I stood and watched the car until I couldn't see it any more.

Needing to pull myself together for the flight home, I decided to change into some more comfortable shoes – we had come straight from dinner and I still had my heels on. I unzipped my case to find the Havaianas flip flops he had bought for me. Inside the bag with them was the business card from the restaurant, when I had asked him to write me a love note. He must have slipped it into the bag without me noticing – he's so good at thoughtful little surprises like that. I read the note and felt happy again. I had seriously had the most romantic weekend I'd ever had with him, so was that it? Would we be OK now? Was all the madness over? Although I was leaving him, I felt the happiest I'd been in a very long time. Finally, my beautiful Mr Starship was back!

Acknowledgments

Writing this book has been a real challenge for me; 31 years is a long time and I have a lot of people to thank, not only for helping me with this book, but for being there for me over the years and helping me to get to where I am today. I am really sorry if I have missed anyone off this list, but I could probably do another book made up of just thank yous.

Dad – thank you for your unconditional love and support. You've stuck by me through thick and thin. I am proud to have you as my father, and I love you very much.

Sylvie, Gordon and Kelly Jones – thank you for looking after me when I was younger. I will never forget what you did for me.

Thank you to my precious little girl, Madison. I am very proud of you and I love you very much.

Nanny Linda – you're a very special lady, thank you for always being there for me.

Joan, Brian and Matthew Dixon and Mary Campbell – thank you for welcoming me into your family and for all the help and support since having Madison. I appreciate it more than you will ever know.

To the rest of my family – Dad's wife Karen; my brother and sisters; cousins Frankie and Joey Essex, Scarlett and Summer Sims, Carly, Nikki, Tony, Keeley and Jonny Davis; Uncle P; Uncle Don and Mauren Tovey, my Godmother – I love you all lots.

Loved ones no longer with us, but always in my heart – Auntie Tina Essex (nee Sims), Nanny Daisy Sims and Godfather Frankie Tovey.

My best friends: Ellie thank you for being the kind of friend you could only dream of; Helen Wolf, best friends since we were 13, you are my oldest friend – love you always; Lauren Pope, AKA Pops, it's been intense and you have become one of my best friends – I love you Pops, and Craig Johnson-Pass, not only are you one of my best friends, you are my manager as well, thank you for putting up with me!

I'd like to thank my other close friends from over the years; Krystal, Marion, Mike Spencer, Ann French, James 'diags' Bennewith, Mikey Kardashian, Joey Bambi, Vas J Morgan, Heidi, Kerry, Jaime Jay (Douglas and family), Jamie Taylor and Tracey.

My management team – Emma Hadley and Craig Johnson-Pass – from Unleashed PR. Thank you for everything you have done so far. I don't know what I would do without you. We really are a great team work-wise, but I also see you as close friends. Thank you for giving me the opportunity to write this book, and I am excited about all the big things we have planned for the future. Go Team Unleashed!

Thank you to my ghost writer, Alice Walker, for putting my life into words and working around my crazy schedule. I really appreciate all your hard work and patience.

I am so pleased to have been given this amazing opportunity to share my life with everyone. Thank you to all at John Blake Publishing for such a speedy turn around and for having faith in my story. A personal thank you to my editor Sara Cywinski; you really have put a lot of time and energy into this book, as well as being really patient with me.

James Marlin and Jenna Aarons, thank you for making one of my dreams possible – my online boutique (www.starshipboutique.com).

Thank you to all the other people I work with, including Natasha Rigler from *Reveal Magazine*, Ashley Moore, Harry Pseftoudis and Andy Le Sauvage. And to all the other magazines, brands and newspapers I have worked with over the past two years, thank you also.

To all of the cast and crew from *TOWIE* thank you for being great people to work with. It has been an amazing journey. Special mentions to Shirley Jones, Gyles Neville, Mike Spencer, Dani Ellis, Genna Gibson, Mark Challender, Emma Bunning , Ruth Wrigley and Tony Wood. Also thank you to Gary Smith at the ITV press office.

Last, but definitely not least, thank you to the love of my life, my Starship. I love you always.

Resources

Mind – the mental health charity
For confidential information and support contact: the Mind Infoline on 0300 123 3393, email info@mind.org.uk, go to the website: www.mind.org.uk or visit your local Mind

Beat – UK charity supporting people affected by eating disorders
For information and support visit www.b-eat.co.uk or contact the helpline on 0845 634 1414

Bullying UK – the nation's anti-bullying support and advice charity.
For free help and support ring the helpline on 0808 800 2222, or visit www.bullying.co.uk for email support services and live advice online.